THE FAULT DOES NOT LIE WITH YOUR SET

The First Forty Years
of Houston Television

by

Jack Harris, Jack McGrew, and Paul Huhndorff

CONTRIBUTORS

TOM REIFF, FRANK Q. DOBBS, PHIL ARCHER, JACK CATO, GARY JAMES, RON STONE, LOIS FARFEL STARK

EAKIN PRESS ★ Austin, Texas

*This history is respectfully and gratefully
dedicated to*

Governor William Pettus Hobby
and
Mrs. Oveta Culp Hobby

*without whose courage, wisdom, and foresight
it would never have happened.*

From 1949 until mid-1953, Channel 2 was the only television station in the Houston area. This led to some major problems — especially for the telephone system and Southwestern Bell.

During the first two years of Houston television there were a lot of technical failures, as expected. But, since there was no alternate broadcast facility, whenever the signal transmitted by Channel 2 faded or disappeared, the first audience assumption was that something was wrong with the television set. Then the telephone exchanges would begin to overload with people calling either the station switchboard or their nearest repairman.

The answer provided by Channel 2 was to display a visual sign and to have an announcer repeatedly read the declaration: "We are experiencing temporary technical difficulties. The fault does not lie with your set. Please stand by."

After the cable arrived and Houston television also included network programming direct from the East or West Coast, there were still periodic gremlins. But the phrase changed.

When it was the network's technical trouble, Channel 2 would display one of a variety of cartoon illustrations and the announcer would say, "We are experiencing temporary network transmission difficulty (or interruption). The fault does not lie with your set . . . or with this station. Please stand by."

Please read and enjoy . . . and remember, "The fault does not lie with your set."

Contents

Prologue

TOM REIFF

Several dedicated broadcasters who helped build this station have now made another contribution to it: this history of KPRC-TV, Houston's Channel 2.

This narrative contains some straight historical information, some "horror" stories, some humorous stories, some poignant stories, some insights, and some strictly personal opinions. It is a look at the standards set and observed by those broadcasters. These pages will give an idea of how we became what we are, and what we must do to continue.

There is no question that George Santayana was right about either learning from the past or having to relive it. Some of our past has been forgotten. This book will keep us from losing more.

Without being portentous, we think the young members of our staff are in for a few shocks and a good deal of hard work during their careers. They will also have a number of opportunities to make continuing contributions to the growth of a great city, to learn from some bright teachers, and, most important, to use their talents and polish their skills in the best imaginable environment.

If all this sounds like a typical "you-people-ain't-got-no-idea-what-it-was-like-in-the-good-old-days" point of view, remember that today is tomorrow's yesterday. What happens today is the history that, if forgotten, must be relived. I hope we will leave future broadcasters something to shoot for — just as these dedicated broadcasters left for us.

In the Beginning

JACK HARRIS

The date was January 1, 1949, an historic moment. People scattered all over southeast Texas were gathered intently around small, blue-lighted portholes cut into huge wooden cabinets. They were anxiously awaiting the appointed hour of 6:00 P.M., when the dim and fuzzy image on the porthole was supposed to come to life and begin to move and speak.

The appointed hour came and went, and still the image did not begin to move. There was no sound except a high-pitched and unwavering tone. The people waited, gathered around some 2,000 of the strange devices with the bluish light.

Finally, at just about 9:30 that winter night, the light began to flicker and a voice came from the speakers in the cabinets: "There's been trouble, plenty of trouble!"

The quavering voice belonged to young broadcast engineer Paul Huhndorff, and with those frustrated words, Channel 2, the first television station in Houston and one of only twelve television stations in the United States at the time, was on the air. It was not an auspicious beginning, but it had been a long time coming.

Any history of television, either as an industry or from the perspective of an individual station, must begin with radio.

The first practical use of the spectrum of broadcast frequencies was for transmission of sound. First came the monotone of an oscillator, broken into long and short bursts, which translated into dots and dashes of the Morse code used by telegraphers to send messages over land lines since the 1840s.

1

Then came voice transmission, combining the new "wireless" technique of Marconi with that of Alexander Bell's telephone. In fact, the microphone used by early radio experimenters was a glorified telephone mouthpiece, and the earphones were slightly modified magnet-and-diaphragm telephone receivers. Finally, some imaginative operators, including a few enthusiastic amateurs, put a microphone in front of the speaker horn of a hand-cranked phonograph — and radio was born.

One of those early amateur enthusiasts was Houston gadgeteer Alfred Daniel, who had been a wireless telegraph instructor of student pilots at Ellington Field during World War I. He set up a wireless rig in his garage on Missouri Street. But Daniel and the other pioneers were almost immediately silenced. The federal government was disturbed by a rapid proliferation of such freelance operations because they were creating chaos in the "ether," interfering with communications between ships at sea and their land bases. New regulations shut down the independents by requiring broadcasters to secure licenses from the Department of Commerce, then headed by Herbert Hoover.

At the same time, American businessmen, always looking for opportunity, were considering the new medium as a vehicle for promotion. Some newspaper publishers saw radio as a circulation-building device, perhaps by offering a simple "crystal set" as a premium to new subscribers.

In Houston, William P. Hobby, governor of Texas during World War I, then publisher of the *Houston Post Dispatch,* persuaded his associates that a radio station was just what Houston and the newspaper needed. So, on May 9, 1925, under a license issued by the Bureau of Navigation, Department of Commerce of the United States, and signed by Hoover himself, radio station KPRC began broadcasting as Houston's first and, for several years, only radio station. Among the station's employees were supervisor G. E. "Eddie" Zimmerman, and, as program director, the same Alfred Daniel of Missouri Street, who stoutly maintained the call letters KPRC stood for "Kotton Port, Rail Center."

As in other major cities and towns, radio in Houston rapidly became a full-fledged mass medium, first rivaling then surpassing the newspapers' ability to deliver audience.

KPRC continued to lead the way, even becoming part owner of one of the two early rival radio stations for a time. Network radio came to Houston through KPRC's affiliation with both the Red and the Blue networks then operated by the National Broadcasting Company (NBC). The Blue network would eventually become ABC, the American Broadcasting Company. The Red network grew into today's NBC, and since it broadcast the day's most popular programs, KPRC chose to stick with NBC. The station was one of the first in the U.S. to establish its own full-time news department, in a time when even the national networks were just beginning news programming.

The boom in radio, both in size of audience and degree of influence, came during World War II. People all over the country depended on radio for immediate news of battles. Both the attack on Pearl Harbor and the D-Day invasion of Normandy were first announced to the nation as radio bulletins. Radio enabled wives and mothers and sweethearts to keep track of the war their men were fighting on both sides of the world.

Radio also provided the entertainment that, momentarily at least, relieved the tension and anxiety gripping the country. Programs offered the inspiration to keep alive the courage and dedication on both the home front and in the combat zones. Great efforts were made to provide radio to the men at war. The new medium's brightest stars, entertainers such as Bob Hope and Bing Crosby, helped by making appearances in battle areas and broadcasting their shows to the folks back home.

The necessities of wartime radio broadcasting created first the portable wire recorder and then the magnetic tape recorder, and made on-the-scene voice reports possible from the tops of London landmarks during the Blitz campaign and from the deck of the Battleship *Missouri* in Tokyo Bay, when the Japanese surrender was signed.

Radio news truly came of age, and a whole generation of voices became familiar to American households. Later, television would match those voices with faces that would become even more familiar.

Before the war, the possibility of sending images by the newfangled radio waves was already on the minds of scientists and engineers. In theory, it was a logical step. If a series of very fast variations or modulations could be superimposed on the radio waves to be converted by a receiver into voice and music, then it seemed possible to modulate the signal with varying impulses that could be translated into pictures.

Turning the theory into fact was more difficult. The first flickering signs of success were not very encouraging. Early experimenters used scanning discs punctured by a spiral of holes at both the sending and receiving ends of the transmission. This music box-like apparatus produced very poor quality images. The system was cumbersome, and it was extremely difficult to keep the discs at both ends of the signal in synchronization.

A different system, using a completely electronic approach, "painted" a picture with a charged particle beam on the inside of a large vacuum tube coated with a phosphorescent material. The motion of the beam, with variations in intensity, was controlled by a series of electronic pulses that could be transmitted just like radio signals. This idea proved much more practical than the spinning discs, but work on the system was halted by wartime demands for engineering skills and scarce materials. Much of the television research, however, was used in helping to perfect one of the Allies' secret weapons — radar.

At the end of the war, experimenters renewed their efforts to perfect the electronic picture system. NBC and CBS started test stations in New York City, broadcasting a few hours each day. People in the New York area began putting receiving antennas on rooftops and staring for hours at the flickering images on the porthole-shaped picture tubes.

The Federal Communications Commission (FCC), successor to the Federal Radio Commission, planned to have television development take place primarily in a portion of the radio-wave spectrum designated as Very High Frequency (VHF), and had set aside a series of approved frequencies, numbering them channels 1 through 13. However, during the war, the military laid claim to the frequency intended for channel 1. So when the VHF band was opened for television use, only channels 2 through 13 were available.

The Radio Corporation of America (RCA), parent company of the NBC network, and a few other aggressive manufacturers began to produce receivers for the VHF channels. Dr. Peter Goldmark, a scientist working for CBS, was more interested in the Ultra High Frequency (UHF) portion of the spectrum, designated as channels 14 through 83. Goldmark believed color television was imminent and could best be accomplished in the UHF signal band.

Television was the domain of these few corporations, financially able to sustain both development and programming of the new medium. The broadcast signal was restricted to the large population centers around Philadelphia and New York City. Entertainment programming was scarce and generally of poor quality. Motion picture companies were not eager to offer any encouragement to this upstart, but obviously dangerous, potential competitor. In fact, most movie companies chose not to sell their products to television. The American Federation of Musicians even prevented its union members from appearing on television in several cities.

By 1947, two years after the war ended, there were very few local stations in operation and all but one were on the East Coast. In St. Louis, one of the Pulitzer newspapers, the *Post Dispatch,* had put a station on the air.

That year, as general manager of Houston's KPRC Radio, I attended a meeting of NBC radio affiliates in Atlantic City. The keynote speaker was General David Sarnoff, chairman of the board of RCA and a trailblazer from the earliest days of radio. Sarnoff, one of the principal architects of America's system of broadcasting, told the assembled radio managers he believed television was destined to become a stronger medium than either radio or newspapers, perhaps stronger than both combined. He warned that any company then engaged in either the radio or newspaper business would be wise to take a long, hard look at this new development.

Sarnoff's comments struck me with great force. Our company was in both the newspaper and radio business. If television was to become the power Sarnoff was predicting, we had best give some serious thought to taking an active role in its development.

All of the radio managers could readily see the potential for entertainment and information and especially advertising offered by television. We also knew that expanding into the new field was going to take significant long-term financing and would involve substantial economic risk.

I returned from the Atlantic City conference and reported to Governor and Mrs. Hobby. We discussed television's potential and the probable financial commitment involved in building and staffing a television station. We tried to estimate the length of time required to develop a circulation of sufficient size to attract advertisers, how long the proposed station could be expected to lose money, and just how much money might be lost before such an operation became a viable enterprise.

After a series of meetings, we agreed that prospects for the immediate future were not glowing, but we concluded that television would eventually become a vital part of the communications industry. As pioneers in the radio business and civic leaders in the Houston community, Governor and Mrs. Hobby decided we had to participate.

An application for Channel 4 in Houston, the channel then being recommended for prospective NBC affiliates, was duly prepared and filed for consideration on January 21, 1948. As it turned out, we were more than a little late with our decision.

Several months earlier, a Houston hotel and laundry owner named W. Albert Lee, who had just started his first radio station, had submitted an application for a television construction permit. The FCC had allocated four VHF channels to Houston in its first rush to speed the development of the new medium. The FCC was making virtually automatic grants to any applicant who was unopposed, was not a citizen of another country, and was not a convicted felon.

Lee qualified on all counts and on January 30, 1948, nine days after The Houston Post Company had filed for Channel 4, Lee was issued a permit for Channel 2, to be known as KLEE-TV.

Within a month there were three more applications filed for the remaining television channels assigned to Houston. The applicants included radio station KTRH, owned by the *Houston Chronicle,* which was in turn owned by Houston financier Jesse Jones; radio station KXYZ, owned by flamboyant Houston oil wildcatter Glenn McCarthy; and radio station KTHT, owned by Roy Hofheinz, former Harris County judge.

Under FCC procedures at the time, a combined comparative hearing would be required, since there were now more applications than available channels. This hearing might not be scheduled for months and could take many more months to complete. The rules also permitted the unsuccessful applicants an appeal, and that might delay the granting of licenses for another year or two. Even if the *Post* were one of the successful applicants, we realized we might be forced to wait three to five years before beginning operation.

There was still another dilemma. The FCC was operating under a policy favoring any applicant not identified with a newspaper on the theory that it was encouraging diversity in the market. Both KPRC and KTRH were affiliated with newspapers. The other two applicants were not. At best, this policy would have led to a direct contest between the *Houston Post* and the *Houston Chronicle,* but just as likely, if other applicants entered the competition, both newspapers could well be passed over.

With a big jump on the would-be competition, Albert Lee got his station on the air on January 1, 1949. This was thanks largely to the heroic efforts of his young chief engineer, Paul Huhndorff, and his novice engineering staff. All Paul or any of his people knew about television was what they had read in a technical manual or what Paul had observed on a quick trip to already operating stations along the East Coast. Paul and his team knew radio, but there were lots of differences.

Paul did attend a three-day seminar conducted by General Electric, and he had been given a walking tour of the three networks' New York studios. That was the extent of the available training in 1948 and 1949. In spite of this inexperience, the job got done — and only three and a half hours behind schedule.

The station owner had even less experience. He had been in the radio business for only about a year and his radio operation was still experiencing start-up pains. In his first year of television operation, only about 15,000 receivers were sold in the Houston area. In order to sell any advertising at all, Lee had to keep his rates low, even lower than rates charged by several Houston radio stations. Still, his operating costs were high.

At KPRC and the *Houston Post* we were watching the operation with great interest. Even though he was curtailing expenses by maintaining a minimal operating staff, we estimated Lee was losing about $30,000 a month and we knew he had no major outside interests to absorb such losses for very long. It was no surprise, then, when Governor and Mrs. Hobby learned KLEE-TV might be for sale.

With all of the uncertainty surrounding the *Post*'s own application for a VHF channel, we decided to try to purchase Lee's television station. We were told the price was $743,000, and in 1950, that was a lot of money, especially for a new business operating deeply in red ink. KLEE-TV's physical assets were quite modest: studios and offices housed in a quonset hut on leased land, a few cameras and related equipment, a transmitter, a tower, and an antenna.

In discussing the prospect with Governor and Mrs. Hobby, I said we should expect at least another $250,000 in operating losses before we could get the station to the break-even point.

Several of their highly placed political and business friends were urging the Hobbys not to pay this extraordinary price for a television station. These people were confident we would be one of the winning applicants when new television construction permits were granted. Looking objectively at the situation, we realized there would surely be protracted FCC hearings over a span of years and the very real possibility, despite assurances, was that the *Houston Post* would not be granted a permit. Purchase of the existing station was the only guarantee, and that became our decision: to buy KLEE-TV, Channel 2.

In late spring of 1950 our request for assignment of license was filed with the FCC. This created open dismay among the other applicants for television channels in Houston. They knew we had the jump on them in a big way.

The application was approved. The Houston Post Company assumed ownership of the station on June 1, 1950, and on July 3, the call letters were changed to KPRC-TV.

We found good news and bad news when we took a close look at the new acquisition. The best news was the superb group of engineers under Paul Huhndorff. Paul had already proved to be an original thinker and he had assembled a staff of excellent, dedicated professionals. These men were producing high quality images and had managed to keep the station on the air in spite of the frequent "gremlins" that were part and parcel of early television.

On the other hand, the sales department, hamstrung by the almost nonexistent audience they were able to offer prospective advertisers, had made all kinds of desperation, cut-rate deals.

We borrowed salesmen from our radio station to solve this problem. These men were already familiar with our policies and requirements and could represent the new owners and operators without confusion or embarrassment.

Terry Lee, a former advertising executive then serving as manager of radio station KXYZ, was brought in to head the new sales department. After a year on the job, Lee left the station to join a major national advertising agency, and we named Jack McGrew sales manager for both radio and television. Fortunately, McGrew had established a reputation with advertisers and advertising agencies in Houston and throughout Texas as a man of the highest caliber. His presence and the reputation he had brought to KPRC Radio guaranteed immediate acceptance of KPRC-TV in the all-important area of advertising.

The firm and guiding hand of Jack McGrew had much to do with both the spectacular early growth and the long-term reputation for innovation and integrity earned by Houston's Channel 2. He literally had to invent a system as he went along, and he did it well.

The program department was about as good as those in most local stations of the time. There was no training ground for television programmers. Everybody was learning as he went along, mostly through trial and error. Motion pictures and live theater were of no real help in the training process. Theatrical companies could rehearse for weeks before the curtain went up. In the Hollywood studios the director could call for take after take until the performance was letter-perfect. Television in 1950 had no such luxuries.

Even radio, where we had talented and experienced performers, was of limited use in figuring out the new medium. Still, the radio station's program manager was to become program director of KPRC-TV as well, and I became general manager of both the radio and television stations. We started slowly, groping our way along, seeking formats and program ideas that were both practical for our limited facilities and appealing to viewers. The Houston area audience, perhaps because it had no alternatives, responded remarkably well to what was something less than sensational entertainment.

The one area where we could use our expertise to immediate advantage was news, and we moved very quickly in that department. Radio news director Pat Flaherty and his assistant, Ray Miller, were assigned to produce a regular schedule of television newscasts.

From a strictly business standpoint, we were pleased that we incurred no losses, on an operating basis, for the first month. By October of 1950, just four months after taking over the operation, KPRC-TV became profitable on its own, including depreciation. Surprisingly, we had not used any of the $250,000 operating cushion.

This quick turnaround in our fortunes was, I think, principally due to the favorable community image of both the *Houston Post* and KPRC Radio. Both the public and the business community had confidence we would do the job right, especially when both the *Post* and KPRC Radio started to vigorously promote television.

We organized a special trade fair at the Plantation Club on South Main Street. The city's retail television set dealers put their latest models on display, and Channel 2 provided entertainment for the big event and a demonstration of how television worked.

The Television Fair was scheduled for the Fourth of July holiday, and more than 50,000 people showed up to have a look at such "name" entertainers as Red Ingles and his "Natural Seven" band, Carol Bruce, June Christy, the Mel Arvin Trio, Gypsy Edwards, and Curly Fox and Texas Ruby. Eleven-year-old Tommy Sands made his television debut that day. Nobody had any idea he would become a national teen idol less than ten years later.

The biggest attraction, however, was the crowd itself. The fair-goers got to see themselves on closed-circuit television while they examined the latest models. It was our first experience with a phenomenon that has proved to be a staple of the business for all these forty years: people like to see themselves on the tube.

Immediately, television receiver sales began to pick up all over the area. The retailers cashed in on a bonanza, but so did the television station. When the call letters had been changed to KPRC-TV, there were 26,000 television sets in use in the market. By December of 1950, six months later, the *Houston Post* reported the number had doubled to more than 53,750. We were most satisfied with our promotional efforts. But we would have been astonished if we had known that by August of 1951, just little more than a year after the station had started operating as KPRC-TV, there would be more than 100,000 sets in use in the area, and that within another year that number would jump to 200,000, with KPRC-TV still the only station in the market.

For the newly combined operation of KPRC Radio and KPRC-TV in July of 1950, we had a staff of sixty-eight people. That included on-the-air announcers, as well as employees in sales, engineering, news, programming, and management. Most of the entertainers were on a contract basis. Many on the staff did double duty, working both radio and television. We felt it was more necessary than ever that radio do well. Radio revenue was expected to help support the early television operation.

Television grew so rapidly, however, that within three months KPRC-TV was standing on its own, and in less than a year, it far outstripped radio as a moneymaker. Some of our company managers had been fearful television costs would drain resources from both the radio station and the newspaper. It just didn't happen.

I had been more optimistic about television than just about anybody in Houston, but even my crystal ball had been cloudy when it projected the potential. In the early schedule planning, I had anticipated hours of operation would be from 2:00 P.M. until 11:00 P.M., and it had been our publicly announced promise to deliver that schedule by the fall of 1950. We easily kept that promise.

I had also foreseen that television would become a serious competitor for radio in the evening hours, but that radio would remain the dominant medium during daytime hours until 5:00 P.M. or so. I expected this mix would be the audience pattern for several years. Many other managers and operators agreed. We couldn't have been further from the truth.

Even the networks followed the conservative logic and only programmed during the evening hours. All network programming was delivered to Houston by kinescope, a clumsy system that photographed images from the TV screen onto black-and-white motion picture film. These kinescopes didn't reach KPRC-TV until several days and frequently weeks after the original live East Coast telecast.

One advantage KPRC-TV did have was the ability to pick and choose from the best network programs. As the only station in town, we were eagerly sought after for affiliation by all four major networks: NBC, CBS, ABC, and Dumont.

Our lineup of stars included Sid Caesar, Imogene Coca, Jack Benny, Milton Berle, Bob Hope, Groucho Marx, Danny Thomas, and Red Skelton. We telecast the Arthur Godfrey Show, the Jackie Gleason Show, and Gary Moore. Dean Martin, Jerry Lewis, Phil Silvers, Perry Como, and Ed Sullivan all appeared on Houston's Channel 2. We had all the great stars in those early days, still remembered by many as the "golden age" of television.

Television drama was creating some surprising works. Hollywood's biggest movie stars either considered television beneath them or were forbidden by contract to appear in this new upstart medium. No such barriers existed for the stars of the Broadway stage, and most production then originated in New York. These performers found a familiar environment. Productions were live and began when the curtain went up (or when the red signal light on the camera was turned on) and continued with only commercial interruptions until the curtain fell on act 3 and the red camera light was turned off.

Just as on the stage, when mistakes were made, cues were missed, or an actor "went up" in his lines, it was all there for the audience to see. Some of the early live mistakes or "bloopers" have gone down as great moments in popular history. There was little rehearsal time, no trial runs out of town to polish the performances or the scripts. What happened when the camera light came on was what the audience saw and, remarkably enough, appreciated.

The men and women who had been well known along "the great white way" of Broadway's lighted marquees suddenly became household words all across the country, and they loved it. Television began to create its own stars and its own star vehicles, among them "Playhouse 90" and "Studio One." "Philco Playhouse," "Westinghouse Theatre," and "G.E. Theatre" reintroduced the classics and created new and powerful works as written by some of America's finest writers. Actors such as Jack Lemmon and Charlton Heston made their first major appearances in these shows, then took their place among the nation's most popular stars.

Dinah Shore, an old family friend who had grown up on the same block with me back in Tennessee, rivaled comedienne Lucille Ball for the title of "Queen of Television."

But network offerings didn't fill up all of the hours in Houston's television day. Film programs, except for syndicated offerings like "The Cisco Kid" and "Hopalong Cassidy," were almost nonexistent. If we wanted to expand our airtime, we had to generate much of our own programming — live studio programming.

There were no accepted formats. There were no approved lists of content. It was up to each station to experiment and find out what worked for the new audience. One early prime-time offering in Houston was "Fashions in Motion," a style show sponsored by Battlesteins, then a major Houston department store. The mistress of ceremonies was Joy Mladenka. She became an almost instant celebrity.

"Talent Shop" featured pianist Johnny Royal, along with Paul

Schmitt and the "TuneSchmitts." Paul Schmitt served as musical director for most of our early live shows, and in one instance barely missed a claim to fame and fortune. A rotund southern gentleman named Tom Parker showed up at the station with his new singing discovery, a young man who mixed country with rhythm and blues. Paul wasn't very impressed. He told "Colonel" Tom Parker that young Elvis Presley was not what television was looking for.

Paul was to later live that episode down by becoming a major participant in the successful career of a fellow Texan named Willie Nelson. Batting .500 isn't bad in any league.

A big local programming success of those early days was "Darts For Dough," a game show adapted from radio and created by our program director, Bert Mitchell. Bob Gray, who later became a successful newspaper and magazine publisher, produced "Most Wanted Men," a video lineup of criminals wanted by the FBI and the Houston Police Department. Ironically, a variation on that early show became one of the hit shows of the late 1980s, this time as a major network offering.

Sports was an early success on Channel 2. Lloyd Gregory, one-time sports editor of the *Post* and a man whose memory of sports facts and figures was encyclopedic, hosted "Sports Talkback."

Without much doubt, the most popular live prime-time show from Houston's KPRC-TV was "Curly Fox and Texas Ruby," featuring Curly and Ruby Fox, recruited from radio, along with radio's Lee Norton as the comic sidekick, "Pancho." This forerunner of "Hee-Haw" was staged in front of a live audience. So were the Friday night wrestling matches, live from the old City Auditorium, with Paul Boesch announcing from ringside.

We had one recurring problem with "Friday Night Wrestling." The show was scheduled for one hour but often ran over. A minute or so was forgivable in those days, but when it became five or six minutes, it really disrupted our evening news programming and we got complaints from both audience and sponsors.

Morris Siegel was the area's wrestling promoter and the producer of the show. Every few months he and I would meet and I would make him promise to end "Wrestling" on time. For the next several weeks, no matter who had whom by the throat, or who was staggering around the ring in an unbreakable "specialty" hold, when Morris signaled the wrap-up from ringside, there was likely to be a dramatic and sudden turnaround in fortune, with the good guy rallying for victory in ten seconds or less. We never seemed to get any audience complaints from the "Friday Night Wrestling" fans.

Daytime hours were left pretty much to each local affiliate. KPRC-TV's top show was, without question, "Matinee," with Houston's "Mr. Television," Dick Gottlieb, as master of ceremonies. The lineup of local talent would never again be equaled in Houston television: Lynn Cole, Marietta Marich, Bobby Lahr (who went on to become a comedy writer for some of Hollywood's biggest names), and another early Channel 2 discovery, Johnny Nash.

There was also baritone Howard Hartman, father of Lisa Hartman, TV star of the 1980s. Don Estes and Jean Hughes were backed up by Paul Schmitt and the "TuneSchmitts" again. But Dick Gottlieb tied it all together and was, without question, the most popular television personality in Houston until the emergence of Ron Stone as today's Channel 2 news anchor and all-around master of ceremonies.

"Matinee" director Bob Marich was always trying to push back the frontiers of live television. One afternoon he saw that Don Estes was scheduled to sing the popular ballad "I Talk to the Trees," so Bob stepped out behind the station and chopped down half a dozen young willow trees. When it came time for Don to start singing, he couldn't find the camera for the trees propped up all over the studio floor. Then he stumbled against a tree support and the forest began to fall.

Another daytime standout in those early days was Jane Christopher's "TV Kitchen," the first and one of the best "how-to-do-it" programs, proving in retrospect that there really isn't anything new under the sun.

Bob Dundas, now an executive with a major advertising agency, got his television start on a show called "Laugh with the Ladies," involving a studio audience interacting with special guests. Mary Beth McDonald presented beauty tips and fashion ideas in a daytime feature we called "Best Foot Forward."

There were, as yet, no soap operas on television. That bulwark of daytime radio did not take over the television day until the advent of videotape, nearly a decade later.

Then, as now, youngsters made up a good part of the daytime viewing audience, especially in the after-school hours. Channel 2 shows included "Howdy Doody," "Kukla, Fran and Ollie," "The Lone Ranger," and "Wild Bill Hickok." Channel 2 also had "Captain Bob," live, in front of an audience of youngsters who were also invited to drop in on Don Mahoney's "Kiddie Corral." There was even a local character dressed like a big drop of milk and, naturally enough, called "Milk Drop Moe." The man inside the huge plastic milk drop was Bobby Lahr.

Baseball was a Channel 2 staple from the start. Ten days after the *Houston Post* assumed ownership of the station, Houston television viewers were shocked to witness a real life-and-death drama played out during the telecast of a Sunday afternoon baseball game at Buff Stadium, where the Texas League Houston Buffaloes played their home games. TV sports was just beginning to develop, and press-box facilities didn't include room for the men and equipment from the upstart competitor. Channel 2's play-by-play announcer and the "cover" camera had been set up in a roped-off row of seats high behind home plate. A second camera had been positioned along the first-base line.

Dick Gottlieb, KPRC-TV's man for all occasions, was hard at work describing the game when a man stepped over the rope and sat down beside him. Gottlieb's version of the incident was as follows:

> The man sat down in an empty chair next to me. He sounded drunk when he said, "Dick Gottlieb, I gotta talk to you right now!"
>
> I put my hand over the microphone, motioned him away and said, "Not now, sir." I turned back to look at the game and he pulled my elbow again. He almost pulled me out of my chair, and said, "Dick Gottlieb, I gotta talk to you right now!"
>
> I guess I got mad; mad at the ushers for letting him get up into the roped-off area and mad that he was interrupting the broadcast. I put my hand over the microphone again and said, louder than before, "Not now, sir."
>
> I started describing the play on the field, when, all of a sudden, there was a gigantic explosion. Blood was all over the place. My audio engineer, Lee Bennet, was covered with blood. I had blood on me. There was blood on my scorepad and on the counter in front of me. When I looked around, the man was slumped over the counter, sliding to the floor. The ball players all stopped and turned, staring up toward us.
>
> The cameraman operating the camera at the end of the row,

to my left, maybe ten feet away, said to the director on his talk circuit, "A man just shot himself here."

The director in the truck downstairs, Gene Osborne, said, "Let's see it," and the camera turned in my direction. For maybe five or ten seconds the picture of the man was on screen.

Stadium employees quickly carried him to an emergency vehicle, and we managed to get the game under way again. I did finish the telecast, but didn't feel very good. They gave me some smelling salts. I didn't think I needed them, but maybe it helped. And they tell me that for a minute or two, right after the gunshot, I kept saying to my wife, over the air, "I'm all right, I'm all right." I also understand a justice of the peace, watching the game on television, called his office downtown and ruled the incident a suicide without ever leaving home.

The man died en route to the hospital, without regaining consciousness. Police investigators reported he had visited several bars before the game, telling customers in each to be sure to watch the afternoon baseball game because he would be on the telecast. An ironic twist was added to the already bizarre story when newspapers reported the suicide victim's son, a North Carolina resident, had witnessed the suicide on television through a freak long-distance reception of our signal, and was preparing to sue the station for "invasion of privacy"! He, or his attorney, apparently thought better of it, for the threat was never made good.

Fortunately, most television coverage of special events went without major incident. Dick Gottlieb was master of ceremonies for the early telethons and became the spokesman for many of Houston's civic and charitable organizations. He served as Harris County director for the March of Dimes for four years in the 1950s and delivered the keynote address for the organization's national convention. Dick has handled twenty-one telethons in all, including fund-raisers in Amarillo and in Omaha, Nebraska. He also served two terms on Houston's city council and was almost elected mayor.

From the earliest days, Channel 2 had broadcast University of Houston home football games. On September 30, 1950, three months after the station changed hands, KPRC-TV televised the first football game in the new Rice Stadium, then just about the finest football stadium in the nation.

Several times during those first years, Channel 2 would televise an afternoon game from Rice Stadium, then follow up with a night telecast of a high school game from Jeppeson Stadium across town. But since there was still no way to bring in a signal from distant points, and would not be until the coaxial cable system reached Houston, we offered no major league baseball and our college football game coverage could only offer games played locally.

We were doing about as well as could be expected without "real time" network service. The kinescope-delayed broadcasts left a lot to be desired, both in picture quality and timeliness. Some of the shows ran as long as three weeks behind the live performance. With shows like Bob Hope's specials, which had very topical opening monologues and one-liners tied to current events, it was like hearing the jokes twice.

One of early television's greatest flukes happened during KPRC-TV's kinescope era. The station was telecasting a three-week-old kinescope of Kay Kyser's "Kollege of Musical Knowledge" on Wednesday nights from 7:00 until 8:00. Our low-band signal bounced off the ionosphere one Wednesday evening and managed to knock the CBS "Wednesday Night Fights" completely off the air for viewers of Baltimore's Channel 2, WMAR-TV. Suddenly, the people of Maryland found themselves watching a three-week-old rerun, and KPRC-TV in Houston got a banner headline in that Thursday's edition of the *Baltimore Sun.*

Being forced to provide a great deal of local programming, we did manage to develop new talent and present some innovations. We found out a lot about the power of television by accident.

A young city councilman named Louie Welch decided to make a run for the mayor's office in 1952. His prospective opponent was the incumbent mayor, a longtime political power in Houston, Oscar Holcombe. He had been mayor on and off for several terms, and his political maneuvering had earned him the nickname "Old Grey Fox." Holcombe was a formidable opponent, but the young contender had a secret weapon. He showed up at Channel 2 with fifteen minutes of aerial motion picture film and a voice narration, and he wanted to buy air time for a special program.

We sold him the fifteen minutes of air time and he rolled the film. It showed blocks and blocks of paved streets and utility easements in undeveloped areas around the city's fringe. Welch charged that the street and utility developments, paid for with city funds, serviced the adjacent property belonging to Holcombe and his associates and greatly increased the land value. The roads started "nowhere" and went to "nowhere," according to Welch, who called the development an obvious example of political corruption.

Holcombe decided to fight back, using Welch's own approach. He wanted to buy air time for a reply, and he wanted to purchase a specific time. The time in question was the same period normally occupied by the nation's number-one show, "I Love Lucy."

The sales staff handed the problem over to me and I tried to place the rebuttal in a different time period, but Holcombe would have none of it. He had decided the time he wanted was perfect. It was just before the voters would be leaving their homes to go to an evening football game at Rice Stadium, he said, and he expected to draw all of their attention.

Reluctantly, we sold Holcombe the time. But we did everything possible to head off the problems we knew would arise. We installed telephone banks and hired extra staff to handle the expected flood of irate callers demanding to know what had happened to Lucy and Desi and Fred and Ethel.

Mayor Holcombe went on the air, live, and rambled on for the allotted time, never really addressing the charges against him. He did talk about the newly opened Allen Parkway between River Oaks and downtown Houston for nearly twelve minutes.

The telephones started ringing and the calls continued to pour into the station for more than an hour after the mayor's moment in the limelight. We had simply delayed all regular evening programming for the fifteen-minute period, but for the faithful viewers, that was not enough. They wanted Lucy, and they wanted her where she belonged.

On the following morning, I received a telephone call from Governor Hobby. He was in the office of Judge James Elkins, a financial and political power of the day and chairman of the board of one of the major banks. Governor Hobby wanted to know how many votes we figured Oscar Holcombe had lost in his television debut.

I reported to the governor and Judge Elkins that the station had logged not hundreds, but thousands of complaints during and after the political telecast.

A few days later the "Old Grey Fox" announced he would not seek re-election. His days in the political arena were over.

But Holcombe's supporters rallied around another, more politically aware candidate. Roy Hofheinz, former Harris County judge, suddenly entered the race with the incumbent's begrudging blessing. Hofheinz had been considering getting back into politics for some time and had become a regular visitor to Channel 2, where he asked very pointed questions of the staff and even prevailed on the late-night crew to let him practice his pitch in front of a studio camera and monitor.

Louie Welch didn't have a campaign strategy in place for this unforeseen set of circumstances. Roy Hofheinz became the new mayor, and Welch bided his time in the wings. He eventually did serve four terms as mayor of Houston and always had a very high regard for the power of television.

With the approach of that 1952 election year, and both the Democratic and Republican national political conventions, we began to apply as much pressure as we could to be able to provide live coverage. We were still the only station in town, and all the networks were anxious to have us interconnected. But AT&T, then the only long distance communications company, had a long list of cities and stations also clamoring for service, and some of them were a good deal closer to network origination points. In fact, the company had us scheduled for service a year later than we were hoping.

Governor Hobby was determined. This would be the first time television covered the national political process with all the attendant hoopla, and the governor wanted KPRC-TV and Houston to be a part of it. He contacted several top AT&T executives and personally pushed for a solution.

One of the original land line links in television was between New York and Atlantic City. That equipment was no longer in use, so the company dismantled the link and brought its components to Texas, where, with some additions, it became the connection between Dallas and Houston.

On July 1, 1952, almost exactly two years after we changed our call letters, we went live for network service. That same day, we began a seventeen-hour broadcast schedule, from 7:00 A.M. to midnight. Only two years before, the station offered only four hours of programming, from 6:00 P.M. to 10:00 P.M.

On July 7 we began live network coverage of the Republican National Convention, and two weeks later, beginning July 21, we televised the Democrats' meeting. Since we were affiliated with all three networks covering the conventions, and since they and their advertisers were anxious to reach the Houston market, we rotated coverage, hour by hour, among the three networks. This resulted in some confusing situations, because switchovers from one network to another were handled by AT&T strictly according to the clock. A speech that began on one network often concluded on another. Similarly, a commercial advertising one product sometimes wound up back-to-back with another spot advertising a competitive product on the next network in the rotation. Home appliance manufacturers were sponsors on two of the networks, and on one occasion a switchover occurred midway into the commercials; viewers saw what appeared to be one commercial extolling two different brands of refrigerators.

The important thing, however, was that Houstonians were able to witness this important step in the American political process. The experience heightened interest in government and provided a vivid demonstration of the importance of television in developing a fully informed electorate.

Interconnection by coaxial cable made it possible for Houston viewers to not only watch regularly scheduled network programming at the same time as the Eastern Seaboard audience, but also, for the first time, to see programs clearly, without the often hazy kinescope image. And in September 1952, Houston viewers, whether sports fans or not, were enthralled by the annual fall spectacle of baseball's World Series, immediately followed by live telecasts of college football. Television no longer had to be sold to the audience. From this point, it did its own selling.

The NBC network had already started expanding its schedule outside the prime-time hours of 6:30–10:00 P.M., into what became known as "late fringe." The first foray into this area was "Broadway Open House," with Jerry Lester and Morey Amsterdam as hosts. In 1954 it was succeeded by the "Tonight Show." Most television fans today associate this long-running classic with Johnny Carson, but Johnny is the third "permanent" host to keep people up past their bedtime. First was Steve Allen, the multi-talented pianist, composer, and humorist, who presided over a staple of artists and performers, including Steve Lawrence and Edye Gorme (who had been introduced to each other by Allen). Next in line was Jack Paar, a sometimes controversial satirist and part-time philosopher. Then finally, Johnny Carson, who has headlined the show longer than the others together.

A companion piece to the "Tonight Show," but at the opposite end of the schedule, was "Today," inaugurated January 14, 1952, by Sylvester "Pat" Weaver, then president of NBC and the most innovative broadcaster the industry has ever seen. Early-morning television, where stations had attempted it, usually consisted of cartoons for kiddies, exercise programs for ladies, and a "ghetto" for alleged public service programs.

Pat undertook "Today" as a major gamble, against advice and dire warnings of experts. It succeeded far beyond the expectations of even its creator. The first host was Dave Garroway, who had made a name for himself as master of ceremonies of "Wide Wide World." At one time or another "Today" has been a showcase for some of television's top talents. And, of course, it was copied, with varying degrees of success, by both of the other networks. Some time after its inaugural, Pat Weaver told me he perceived "Today" as a program people didn't need to watch, but instead, like radio, could listen to while shaving, preparing breakfast, or going about their morning routine.

During the first two years The Houston Post Company operated Channel 2, we substantially improved its facilities. Still, the quonset hut behind Pin Oak Stables was less than adequate. KPRC Radio's offices and studios had been on the mezzanine floor of the Lamar Hotel, downtown at the corner of Main Street and Lamar, since the early 1930s. We determined to combine the two operations under the same roof. I sat down with Paul Huhndorff to start planning the move. We didn't want to be plagued by the same "alligators" that had made the start-up at the original studio such a cliffhanger.

The Alligators

PAUL HUHNDORFF

It was never an ambition of mine to be "on the air," and even though I managed to inaugurate television programming in Houston with my unrehearsed and somewhat less than polished announcement of trouble in the studios, I was not thrilled with the distinction. However, as the years passed, it began to take on a certain importance, and as Channel 2 expanded service and prospered, I was able to take a certain pride of accomplishment in the way we handled the "alligators" that made those early days so miserable for the engineering staff.

"Alligators" was Jack Harris's term for all of the difficulties that often led to the sign on the home screen that read, "The Fault Does Not Lie With Your Set." During the first year after The Houston Post Company bought Channel 2, there were plenty of those occasions. Harris was running the radio station from offices downtown in the Lamar Hotel on Main Street and driving out to Post Oak every day around noon for a meeting with the TV staff.

During one of those early meetings he told a story originally written by New York humorist and newspaper columnist Dorothy Parker. She had hired a new maid and was planning a party for the evening of the maid's first day on the job. Just as Parker was leaving her apartment to go to the newspaper office, the mailman delivered a package from Florida. Inside was a tiny live alligator of the kind often sold as a tourist souvenir in those days. She was in a hurry, so she placed the alligator in the bath tub, ran a little water, and left.

When she returned late in the day, the apartment was a mess. The maid had obviously done nothing. Pinned to the bathroom door was a note: "Miss Parker, I quit. I cannot work any place where alligators are kept in the bathroom. I would have told you before but I never thought the subject would come up."

Jack Harris was determined that all of the subjects would come up. The meetings usually revolved around programming ideas and discussions of how to avoid or correct all of the "alligators" that had made the previous day's programming less than perfect. Believe me, there was plenty to talk about.

It's true that we knew next to nothing about television when we started installation of KLEE-TV in the summer of 1948, but that wasn't so bad. Virtually no one knew any more than we did about this new business. Everybody was proceeding on trial and error.

Our state-of-the-art facility started with one GE studio camera with an optical viewfinder, not too different from the then popular Kodak Brownie snapshot camera. We installed two GE Iconoscope film cameras, two Bell and Howell 16-millimeter film projectors to handle the kinescope programming, a GE console switching unit, and a standard GE audio console. Having experience in radio, we had the audio system figured out. As for the rest of it, we dived right in and established a learning curve.

During the first days of KLEE-TV, we spent about three hours every morning just to "count down" the sync generator that insured that all phases of the video transmission were in step. Then we would begin telecasting with the test pattern and an audio tone while we fine-tuned the system. We had been transmitting the test pattern for eleven days before we officially began programming on January 1, 1949. Everything seemed to be in fine shape.

But there was an "alligator" at work in the cooling system of the transmitter. The system was made up of a series of water lines or coils manufactured out of a new plastic called Saran, and you were supposed to be able to handle the stuff just like copper tubing but without the danger of accidental electrocution. As we neared our official 6:00 P.M. sign-on fanfare on that fateful evening, one of the Saran cooling lines burst. Water started spraying all over the inside of the equipment cabinets, and we had to shut down.

We put some people to work bailing out the waterlogged transmitter, and some others to try to patch the line. The new plastic just wouldn't hold. The 6:00 P.M. air time came and went. I got a refrigeration company on the telephone and they provided us with some old-fashioned copper tubing. The water leak was stopped, but then we had to re-engineer the insulation system. Copper is an excellent conductor of electricity, and the transmitter was driven by several thousand volts of the stuff. If the copper tubing had come into contact with any part of the power grid, someone could have been killed or badly injured and the whole plant might have burned down.

We did the best we could. We double-checked the jury-rigged cooling system and we crossed our fingers. Then, at 9:30, I was appointed to tell the viewers why we had missed the boat.

I wound up doing a lot of explaining as time went on. Jack Harris decided it would be a good idea to offer a regularly scheduled program designed to help viewers get the most from their new device. We called the show "Television Roundtable" and I was the host, offering tips on television reception and adjustment.

The station's first signal tower, located right beside the quonset hut studios, was all of 500 feet tall. It was black iron and supported a GE antenna that radiated video signal strength of fifteen kilowatts. Our signal covered a radius of about fifty miles.

The small studio was lit with banks of photo floodlights mounted on sheets of plywood and supplemented by a few 750-watt Kliegl spots. We mounted a small light on the camera to highlight the performers' eyes. This little number was called a "Rink Dink," and I've always wondered which came first — the Rube Goldberg lighting contraption or the name that became synonymous with "slap-dash" and "half-baked."

Early television cameras couldn't deal with shadows. In order to eliminate them, we poured on the light. The banks of incandescent lights put the temperature at substantially above tolerable; however, costs had to be held in check, according to Albert Lee, so there was no air conditioning. Only on the coldest days of that first winter were performers and technicians able to stand the heat of the studio for more than short stretches of time. In fact, as another cost-cutting measure, the engineers and other staffers were assigned rotating duties of sweeping and mopping the floors before each day's telecast started.

One of the things we did right from the beginning was to put together a mobile unit. It was a Lynn Coach, actually built along the lines of an intercity bus and just as heavy. In fact, after we had installed the required equipment, including two Dumont Image Orthicon remote cameras, the coach was so loaded down the rear axle kept breaking. We kept a stack of spare axles on hand but, at one point, the problem got so bad we were pulling the mobile unit around town with a heavy-duty wrecker.

Being towed around to various special events while facing backward didn't do a lot for remote crew morale or the station's image. Still, that old coach got the job done and established Channel 2 in Houston as one of the major remote telecast facilities in the country. We're still proud of that distinction.

Working those remotes led indirectly to some other firsts for Channel 2. To transmit the signal from remote site to the station for telecast, we bolted a microwave dish to the side of the tower. One of my jobs was to climb the tower and adjust the receiving dish each time we did a new remote. That got old in a hurry during the cold, wet winter of 1949, so we designed and built our own dish control system, operated remotely from inside the studio. To make the system work, we rigged two war surplus aircraft prop pitch motors to the dish and ran the control wires into the building. That method worked fine, and it encouraged us to try even more elaborate self-help projects as time went on.

Looking back, it seems so primitive — sort of the log cabin stage of television — but those were exciting days. When The Houston Post Company bought the station, the operation began to really pick up steam. The first major purchase was air conditioning, and we were so glad to have it that the engineers pitched in and built the foundation for the new unit. Next, janitors were hired. Now that everybody had a clear-cut job description, morale went way up.

The Hobbys planned on an expanded operation from the very first day. Within a few months there was already discussion of a new and bigger facility for KPRC-TV. The first idea was to combine both the radio and television stations by adding a much larger quonset hut next door to the original studio building. The landowners, the Abercrombie family, weren't interested in selling any of the property around the Pin Oak Stables. The Hobbys weren't interested in building on leased land, so a search for a new station site was started.

The chosen location was only about a mile north of the original station building, and still on Post Oak Road. It was a larger parcel of land than we needed, but the price was right and it looked good as a long-term investment. The new and larger quonset hut had already been ordered by the time the decision was made to move, so we were stuck with the design concept. A two-story, L-shaped brick building housing radio studios and offices was built to stand in front and to one side of the quonset hut studios. A one-story, flat-roofed metal addition across the back of the complex would house props and, eventually, a new transmitter room. This arrangement left an open atrium in the center of the structure. We planned to make this our "outdoor" studio.

Early television inherited many things from radio. One was the glass-enclosed booth housing the director, the producer, and assorted technicians. From this seat of power, the occupants could look out over the entire studio and position the performers to best advantage — or so the theory went. In any event, that's the way it had always been done in radio.

True to tradition, Channel 2's first studio in the quonset hut behind Pin Oak Stables had the glass-fronted director's booth, positioned on the second level so that the producer and director and other staffers could look out over the studio without having their view blocked by cameras, sets and props, camera operators, floor managers, or performers.

In the same tradition, each studio in the new plant up the road on Post Oak had its own director's booth, with a broad expanse of glass looking out over the studio. There was also a sponsors' booth above the director's booth, equipped with two rows of theater seats, affording its occupants a wide-angle bird's-eye view of the entire studio. (Each studio also had an announcer's booth, set off to one side of the director's booth, with glass facing both the director's booth and the studio, for the use of an off-camera announcer.)

But after all this expensive design and construction, we realized the ability of the director and producer to see all of the activity on the studio floor was much more a handicap than a help — that it actually distracted their attention from the pictures on the monitors that enabled them to select the sequence of shots to be broadcast. In short order, the glass front of the director's booth was covered and the group within worked "blind," guided only by what the camera could see. After all, that was all the audience could ever see.

As for the sponsors' booths, they may have been used by paying guests a half-dozen times but soon lost out to master control room expansion. Sponsors, we discovered, prefer to see the program as their customers see it, on the television screen.

Construction of the new building had gone without a hitch, but actually moving the equipment into the facility proved to be extremely complicated. The trick was to get it done with a minimum of "off-the-air" time, even though everything in the old building would have to be in place before operation from the new studios could begin.

We drew up an elaborate plan covering the order in which each piece of equipment would be disconnected and loaded for the move up Post Oak to the new building. The plan was very specific. What went on the trucks last was what had to be unloaded first, to insure that the station would be back on the air in the shortest amount of time. All of the connector cables were carefully tagged. There was even a series of technical rehearsals for the big move. As the final day approached, we moved everything that was not essential to keeping the station broadcasting, and we continued to refine our plan for the last minute race against time.

Our viewing audience was told in several promotional announcements about the big move. We explained to the viewers that we would be signing off early on the night of March 19, 1953. We also promised to be back on the air early on the morning of the 20th.

The plan went off well — up to a point. We got the equipment at the old station disconnected and loaded onto the moving vans in the proper order and then set off up the two-lane blacktop road that was then Post Oak. Motorcycle police with flashing red lights preceded the convoy. Station news reporters and a reporter-photographer team from the *Post* were on board, ready to cover the big event.

But this impressive armada, sailing through the night, made no impression at all on a visiting Dallas motorist out joyriding with his girlfriend in the middle of the night. He managed to plow his car head-on into the convoy's leading truck. Luckily, the van was moving very slowly, with station employees standing among the heavy equipment to help steady the load. Still, the sudden stop managed to shift the load, and Fred Reynolds, a burly camera operator, took the brunt of the jolt. Fortunately, neither Fred nor the equipment suffered serious damage.

The driver of the car and his companion were not seriously injured, either, but the psychological shock of being suddenly surrounded by police officers and popping camera flash bulbs and a swarm of irate television engineers must have been substantial.

The wrecked car was cleared out of the way and the convoy moved on. The most ironic part of the whole process was that the trucks were literally preparing for a left turn into the new station when the car appeared on the scene.

There was a lot of adrenalin flowing when the vans were finally unloaded and the equipment wheeled into place and plugged in. When the hour for sign-on was at hand, KPRC-TV, Channel 2 in Houston, was back on the air, and in a new state-of-the-art facility more than three times the size of the first studio. We had no idea that we would start to outgrow that new complex within a dozen years.

In Living Color

JACK HARRIS

From its inception, television had a big edge over other media, both for entertainment and advertising. Television offered sight, sound, and motion. Radio had sound and the illusion of motion; newspapers had sight and, sometimes, color; magazines had sight and color. What early television lacked was color, but that last barrier began to yield on December 21, 1953, with the approval by the FCC of standards for compatible color.

NBC's parent company, Radio Corporation of America (RCA), had been largely responsible for research leading to the FCC's action, and standards adopted were essentially those proposed by RCA. It was only fitting, therefore, that NBC should take the lead in developing color programming. Among the first steps was modification of circuits over which network programs were fed to affiliated stations, and in our case, that took place in the spring of 1954 when the link between Dallas and Houston was upgraded.

On May 3, 1954, NBC fed into its network and KPRC-TV the first color television program, "The Voice of Firestone." There were no color receivers on the market in Houston, and none in Houston's homes. We invited a number of civic and business leaders to our studios, where we did have color monitors. As we expected, the impact was tremendous.

Neither ABC nor CBS was anxious to get into color programming. Costs were substantial, and the audience equipped to receive color was small. NBC confidently claimed the title "Color Net-

29

work," and expanded its color schedule until, in a little more than a year, it had at least one program in color each night of the week.

As part of a color promotion, NBC introduced an animated cartoon peacock with a multi-hued tail as a visual announcement of color broadcasts. The bright bird became a nationally recognized symbol and reminded black-and-white set viewers that they were missing something.

A number of NBC's affiliates urged the network to charge its advertisers a premium for color programs and commercials, citing the precedent set by newspapers and magazines whereby they did charge extra for color. NBC resisted the pressure, arguing that penetration at consumer level was minimal, and advertisers should be encouraged to expand their own use of color. The argument won over skeptics. Advertisers, in effect, got a bargain for a while. The addition of color increased the effectiveness of television advertising so much that advertisers hastened to convert and willingly paid the increased rates that developed over time.

As color audience figures began to rise, ABC and CBS finally began conversion. By the sixties, network color was common. Black-and-white pictures were passé.

KPRC-TV's venture into local color required substantial investments in time and money. For syndicated film programs and film commercials, we needed new color film projection-camera chains. For news film we needed a new color processor. And for live studio work, including news programs, we needed new color cameras and lighting. The final step came in September 1966, when we inaugurated local live programs and film news reports in color.

There have been so many radical innovations in television's relatively short history that the word "revolutionary" has lost its impact. However, the development of magnetic tape recording of both sound and picture does deserve the word. For the first time, it became possible to reproduce, instantly, without recourse to film processing, any program or other visual and aural material.

Again, KPRC-TV was a leader. On February 25, 1958, we took delivery of an Ampex VR-1000 videotape recorder, and became the first station in Texas and the twelfth in the country to be able to offer local tape production. By today's standards, accustomed as we are to the improvements miniaturization has made possible, that old Ampex was a clumsy monster, wider than an executive desk and twice as tall, and subject to all sorts of aggravating problems. But it changed the way we do things to a greater extent than any other piece of television equipment since the camera itself.

From the beginning, Channel 2 specialized in remote originations. A self-contained remote unit was among the first pieces of equipment delivered to KLEE-TV, and even before the station was sold, Paul Huhndorff and his crew had become old hands at pickups outside the studios. Many of those early remotes were sporting events. But this capability led us into network originations on a scale far beyond anything we had ever considered.

In April 1955 we fed NBC two broadcasts of the "Dinah Shore Show" from the main ballroom of the Shamrock Hotel. Channel 2 learned an important lesson from those two broadcasts, and from the origination of the "Tonight Show," with Steve Allen, that same week from the Shamrock Hotel. We found out just how much money a station could lose on network originations. A lot.

NBC felt affiliates should handle assignments at their cost, since it was supposedly an honor to be selected for a network origination. The Shamrock was not properly equipped for such a program, so we first had to add transformers to provide adequate electrical power, then rent lights from a theatrical lighting outfit in Dallas. The network sent us plans for set construction, and we estimated a cost of $300. The sets actually cost almost ten times that amount. Yes, we paid for the education, but we soon put our knowledge to use for our benefit and that of other NBC network stations.

Pro football expansion wars were being fought even back in the 1960s. One element was the American Football League (AFL), then an outlaw but now a respected division of the NFL under the banner of the American Football Conference (AFC). The new league originally made a deal with ABC for Sunday afternoon television broadcasts of its games, but when the arrangement began coming apart, NBC saw its opportunity to compete head-to-head with CBS, which had a longtime exclusive arrangement with the National Football League (NFL).

Under the new NBC-AFL contract, NBC obligated itself to broadcast six games each Sunday afternoon, but the network had neither the equipment nor the manpower to make six widely scattered pickups each week. As chairman of the NBC affiliates, I met with Bob Kintner, then NBC president, and he agreed the network had a problem. With his support, I urged NBC affiliates in each

city with an AFL franchise to secure color remote gear so it could
be leased to NBC for Sunday afternoon football.

Under the proposal, each station would be able to amortize its
investment over a five-year period by charging NBC for use of its
equipment, including cameras, tape machines, and the remote control switching unit. By charging at a rate above actual costs for personnel required to operate the equipment, stations would add to
their capabilities and make a profit. And NBC games would be in
color, something CBS could not yet do, making NBC, its affiliates,
and the AFL more competitive against the older, better established
NFL arrangement. Slightly more than half the affiliates involved,
including KPRC-TV, made the investment in color equipment.

The AFL contract turned out to be an excellent business decision for both the network and the affiliates. It was also a big plus
for the fledgling pro football league. People started tuning in the
AFL games simply for the novelty of watching professional football
in living color. They found they also liked the kind of wide-open
game being played by the newcomers.

Since Channel 2 made a number of NBC pickups in addition
to the Sunday football games, we were able to amortize our capital
outlay in only two years. In fact, at one time during the 1960s the
network reported KPRC-TV was receiving about half the total
number of dollars it was spending with all affiliates for remote originations.

Many of those additional network feeds came from NASA's
huge space installation at Clear Lake, and we were involved from
the beginning. Houston also had its own major league baseball
team playing in the Astrodome, an exciting showplace in its own
right, and NBC had the major league baseball contract.

KPRC-TV became so identified with projects for all three
commercial networks that several of our staff, especially director
Jon Burkhart, were cited for superior work by more than one
group. On Jon's retirement in 1987, the NBC baseball play-by-play
crew went out of its way to pay him special tribute. One of our
audio engineers, Frank Hicks, was twice nominated for an Emmy,
in 1974 and 1975, for his work on the CBS network telecasts of
NBA basketball; another of Channel 2's engineers, Leonard Patillo,
received an Emmy for engineering achievement for his work on the
Nashville "Summer Lights" program in 1987, an annual feature of
our Tennessee sister station, WTVF (TV).

KPRC-TV has always prided itself as being a people company, giving credit and opportunity where it is deserved. Through the years, employee turnover has been much less than is usually associated with the broadcasting business. Most of those who have moved on have been taking advantage of larger opportunities and greater challenges at the network level or in related fields. Still, every large organization will be faced, now and then, with employees who simply don't measure up or fit in.

The KPRC stations have always made an effort to ease the pain of dismissal. Fair severance pay and plenty of notice have been part of company policy. But people are people, and this approach hasn't always worked. One employee who didn't quite measure up was given three months' notice and told that she could use her desk and company time to seek a new job. Three months later she was told that the grace period was over, that it was time to clear out her desk.

"You mean you're firing me?" the offended worker asked in a voice full of outrage.

"No," the supervisor replied. "I'm terminating you. I fired you three months ago."

Another time, the station manager had an ongoing problem with the program director. There was confrontation over every decision: fights with the engineering department and even refusal to support policy directives from the front office.

The program director was able and personable, just not in agreement with the manager's goals. Finally, the manager had all the resistance he could stand, but in the interest of civility, still wanted to be diplomatic.

He called the program director into his office and closed the door. "It must be obvious to you," he said, "that you and I are just not working well together. I know you realize this can't go on. I know I do. I've determined that one of us has to go, and I've decided it's you."

"Why me?" asked the program director in a startled voice.

Thirty-five years later, the manager still has not provided an answer.

Through the years KPRC-TV has continued to originate innovative programming on both the local and national level. One remarkable series was for NBC's "Wide Wide World" with Dave Garroway, beginning in October 1955 and extending into February

1957. This series celebrated television's newly found mobility: the freedom to go anywhere at any time and tell an informative and entertaining story. As one of the best equipped remote facilities in the country, KPRC-TV covered such varied assignments as part of a performance by the Houston Symphony Orchestra, then conducted by Leopold Stokowski; a sequence from the Texas Prison Rodeo at Huntsville; and a tour of Temple Emanu-El, directed by its then rabbi, Robert I. Kahn.

One entire program originated from this area, including pickups from the San Jacinto Monument, the Battleship *Texas*, the Houston Ship Channel, and a shrimp boat in the Gulf of Mexico. We telecast a Roy Rogers performance at the Houston Livestock Show (on Sunday night in prime time for NBC) and a weeklong series of broadcasts of the heartstring-tugging "Queen for a Day."

The experiences gathered with that old Lynn Coach mobile unit being dragged around town by a heavy-duty wrecker were proving to be one of KPRC-TV's strongest assets — that and the willingness to seek out and master challenges with innovative solutions as demonstrated by Paul Huhndorff and his engineering staff.

On the Road

PAUL HUHNDORFF

Mobility is taken for granted in today's television business. Every item in the equipment inventory is designed for reasonable portability. When Channel 2 first committed to the idea, literally nothing was portable. We had to adapt or convert or build from scratch, but we were determined to be able to take our show on the road.

Through the forty years of operation, Channel 2 has originated every conceivable type of remote programming, even a series of special reports transmitted from the Johnson Space Center to Moscow. Ironically, that one was easy compared to some of the early efforts in the days when cameras weighed about a hundred pounds and needed so much light we had to rewire almost every facility in which we mounted a camera.

NBC committed to a weekly news feature show called "Wide Wide World" back in 1955. The concept was revolutionary. Dave Garroway would host the Sunday afternoon show from some location or another and he would either narrate or introduce segments that originated from several areas around the country. This was all live and very seldom rehearsed.

Channel 2's first effort for "Wide Wide World" was telecasting a rehearsal of the Houston Symphony Orchestra, then under the direction of flamboyant and controversial Leopold Stokowski. The "alligators" were at work and we were experiencing some serious camera trouble.

The New York director for the show was feeling the tension

and the frustration. He began to complain about the poor picture quality to our remote engineer, Vernon "Blackie" Black. Very caustically, he questioned Vernon over the headset, "Do you expect me to put a camera that bad on the air?"

Vernon's cool response was "If that was the only camera I had, then I would put it on."

It went on the air — not very good quality — but live from Houston and the Music Hall, and eventually we were forgiven because NBC continued to count on Channel 2's remote facilities as "Wide Wide World" pushed back the frontiers of telecasting.

The Texas Prison Rodeo was fascinating to the rest of the country back in the fifties, so the network decided to make one of the October performances of the "Wildest Show on Earth" a part of Dave Garroway's Sunday afternoon look-see at the country. Tommy Reiff, now graduated to general manager and called Tom, was to make his network directing debut, live from the rodeo arena in Huntsville. Tom called for a camera to be positioned inside the arena, so we dug a hole wide enough for a camera and operator and deep enough for the lens to be at ground level. Right on cue, a wild Brahma bull charged out of the chute and circled in front of the television audience, bellowing and pawing the ground.

Even in these days of videotape and innumerable re-takes, it couldn't have been done any better. And it encouraged the network to continue to look to Texas and Houston's KPRC-TV for the difficult remote assignments. NBC decided to devote an entire episode of the Garroway Sunday show to the Lone Star State. It was called "Texas USA."

We were called on to put a crew on location at the San Jacinto Battleground with instructions to cover both the monument and the Battleship *Texas*. We were also required to rig a camera and a remote transmission dish in a helicopter for a look at the Houston Ship Channel. This idea was being attempted for the first time. It wasn't just the camera and the dish that we were concerned about. Helicopters were just beginning to appear on the scene, and the only ready source was the U.S. Army.

I designed a camera mount for the army's flying machine and volunteered to go up with the camera operator and serve as the microwave dish operator, making sure the transmitter on board stayed lined up with the receiving antenna on top of a ship channel grain elevator.

The camera and the dish worked fine, but when we were flying a quick pre-show dress rehearsal, the helicopter pilot notified us that if he landed, he would be unable to take off again. The machine was only allowed to take off and land a certain number of times before the rotor clutch assembly had to be replaced. There wasn't much choice. We stayed aloft, criss-crossing over the channel and the grain elevator and waiting for showtime.

The fuel held out. The helicopter stayed in the air and the shot of Houston's unique geographic feature was a part of the show.

As long as the network continued to telecast "Wide Wide World," Channel 2 in Houston was a regular part of the program. We set up our mobile unit on Avery Island near New Iberia, Louisiana, for a report on how Tabasco Sauce is made. We transmitted pictures from a shrimp boat off Galveston by placing a receiving antenna on a balcony at the Galvez Hotel and hanging a bright white bedsheet off the balcony railing to serve as a visual target for the microwave dish operator on board the boat.

Like a lot of the solutions we found in those first years, the bedsheet target was crude but effective, and the job got done. Our second official mobile unit, replacing that old Lynn Coach with the fragile axles, was called the "Pie Wagon," so named by an NBC sports director. It lasted until 1962, when it was replaced by a new vehicle and new camera and switching equipment.

The Manned Spacecraft Center at Clear Lake was to be the focus of the American exploration of space, and Channel 2 was destined to play a major role in making the entire country a participant in the suspense and the long string of spectacular successes. We were determined to be up to the task. Videotape was beginning to come into its own, so we equipped a second truck with a low-band RCA two-inch tape machine and thought we'd be ready for anything that came "down the pike" for a long time to come. That "long time" lasted until 1968, when we decided to convert all phases of the operation to color.

This time we wound up with a convoy of vehicles. One truck carried remote color cameras and camera control systems, a second truck was equipped with an RCA videotape machine and a slo-mo disc for instant replay situations, and a third truck became the switching and control center.

Change keeps coming, faster and faster. One of Channel 2's first big achievements was a homemade weather radar system, just about the first in the nation to be operated by a television broadcaster. Along the Texas Gulf Coast, weather is always a major concern, especially during the summer hurricane season. So back in 1954, our confidence buoyed-up by our other handmade successes, we purchased a war surplus navy fire control system and modified it to scan the weather.

That first system had an effective range of about forty miles, not enough to keep track of major storm systems early enough to give accurate warning information. We kept tinkering and modifying and changed the location of the antenna, increasing the effective range to 150 miles.

When Hurricane Carla blew across the coast in September of 1961, Channel 2 was able to track its course early enough and accurately enough to give plenty of warning to area residents who evacuated the low-lying areas by the tens of thousands.

Next, we tracked down a surplus NIKE-ZEUS missile-tracking antenna system, designed to follow the flight of supersonic rockets. Again, it was modified so that its fourteen-foot co-planar antenna increased the practical weather radar range to a radius of 250 miles. We figured we had designed this system to last out the century.

But we hadn't figured on a major fire that destroyed the radar installation in July of 1977. By that time there were several companies in the business of designing and building weather radar systems for television stations all over the country.

We were able to acquire replacement radar that could also read the height of storm cloud formations as they developed. This gave us an ability to monitor the build-up of storm energy and determine the potential severity early enough to give adequate warning anywhere in East Texas or western Louisiana.

In late 1987 we installed a Doppler surveillance system, making it possible for the weatherman to monitor the potential for tornadoes. This improved radar system, which operates on the change of pitch in wind sound, can tell the operator both the directions and the speeds of turbulent wind currents. It is the first unit of its kind in southeast Texas.

Today our radar system is truly state-of-the-art. Tomorrow, who knows? When Channel 2 went on the air in 1949, the equipment inventory ran less than a page. The value of that equipment was about $350,000. Listing station equipment inventory today would require a catalog, and the investment in equipment alone now amounts to about $15 million.

We still maintain one original piece of studio gear, a Mole-Richardson microphone boom, bought brand new in 1949 and still in working order. It is a tangible link with a past that we remember with pride and a reminder of how far we have come.

Whatever is on the horizon — high definition television with wall-sized viewing screens, fiber optic transmission lines, or ideas not yet conceived — we know from the past that Channel 2 will lead the way toward those new horizons.

The News Comes First

JACK McGREW

KPRC-TV's nationally honored news department grew directly out of an already well-established, widely acclaimed KPRC Radio news department. In fact, in the beginning it *was* the KPRC Radio news department. Originally, KLEE-TV had no local news programming. There wasn't even any network television news in Houston. That wouldn't come until cable interconnection in 1952.

KPRC Radio pioneered broadcast news in Texas and the Southwest, beginning in the 1930s, and was one of the earliest radio stations in the country to establish its own local news operation. Among the first KPRC newsmen on the air were Pat Flaherty and Ray Miller. Both men were experienced radio announcers who began their news careers on KPRC. They learned news broadcasting by doing it and went on to teach generations of others.

Flaherty and Miller had their careers interrupted by World War II. Flaherty, after a tour of duty with the Red Cross in the South Pacific, was recruited by NBC as a war correspondent and followed MacArthur from New Guinea to Manila. He was among the first Americans to arrive as the liberators of the infamous Santo Tomas internment camp.

The Japanese had locked up all of the captured U.S. civilians in Santo Tomas after the fall of Manila and Bataan. Among the captives was Bert Silem, NBC Radio's Far East correspondent, who had been filing a voice report from a Manila rooftop when the victorious Japanese army had turned off his power.

Pat Flaherty personally liberated Silem and rushed him

straight back to downtown Manila, where MacArthur's staff was setting up its new headquarters and radio communications facilities. Bert was ushered to a microphone set aside for NBC broadcast back to the U.S. He collected his thoughts for a moment, then when the engineer gave the signal, Bert spoke into the microphone, "As I was saying three and a half years ago when I was so rudely interrupted . . ."

Jack Harris was then serving with MacArthur's headquarters. That moment was his introduction to Flaherty. Neither man had any idea they would soon be working together at Flaherty's old Houston radio station. In fact, Pat turned down an offer to become bureau chief for NBC in Washington to return to Houston.

Ray Miller spent the war years as a submariner in the navy, then, after a brief postwar stint with KPRC, returned to Australia to marry his wartime sweetheart. He founded and directed the news department for Australia's commercial radio service, the MacQuarrie Network. After a couple of years, Ray tired of the bureaucratic government of Australia and returned to Houston with his bride.

With the support of news-oriented owners and managers, news director Flaherty and his assistant, Miller, built KPRC News into one of the top broadcast news organizations in the country. The team earned a national reputation through coverage of such major stories as the Texas City disaster, handled from the scene of the tragedy for NBC, with nineteen network originations over the three-day crisis.

Even in 1950, the new owners and operators of Channel 2 were firmly convinced that news would become one of the most vital services of the medium. They also believed their own radio news staff could develop a television newscast viewers would find informative and interesting. The transition was swift and effective. Flaherty, while serving as news director for radio and television, became one of Houston's most familiar faces as Channel 2's news broadcaster (the term "anchorman" had not yet been coined). His no-nonsense approach to stories earned the station an immediate audience.

Pat was a newsman literally to the end of his days. He suffered a fatal stroke while reporting the 7:45 A.M. newscast for KPRC Radio. Pat's voice faltered. There was a long pause, then another faltering news item and Pat slumped over the microphone. After a long moment of silence, KPRC news reporter, Tom Fox, stepped in and finished reading Pat Flaherty's final report to Houstonians, just the way the pioneering newsman would have insisted it be done.

Determined to stay abreast or ahead of developments in the news field during those early days, Channel 2 introduced significant new equipment and concepts to the Houston market. With Ray Miller as its new director, the television news department developed facilities for live, on-the-scene reporting; it had Houston's first and, for many years, only television weather radar; it was first to introduce videotape to replace film for field reporting; it hired the first black and the first woman reporters in Houston; and was the first television station in the state to establish a full-time, fully staffed news bureau in the capitol at Austin. Barbara Jordan, at that time a state senator, "sold" that idea to station management during a broadcasters' convention.

KPRC-TV also became one of the few stations in the country to offer a simultaneous Spanish translation of its 10:00 P.M. newscast, through arrangements with a Houston radio station. Viewers who had only a limited understanding of English could watch Channel 2 News while listening to a synchronized translation on their radio.

In September 1961, one of the century's most destructive hurricanes struck the upper Gulf Coast. The weather bureau called it "Carla," and for the better part of three days, KPRC-TV virtually abandoned its regular schedule to report the storm's progress, to warn residents of the mounting hazard, and to bring aid and comfort to the storm's victims.

The eye of the storm crossed the coastline in the vicinity of Victoria, but the "hot" quadrant, where the force of counterclockwise wind circulation was at its greatest, passed directly over Galveston Island.

KPRC-TV's radar installation proved its worth. With it, and a constant flow of information from the United States Weather Bureau, we were able to track the giant hurricane with great accuracy. Residents all along the threatened coast were kept fully informed, and our news people were in the right places at the right time. Loss of life and property was kept to a minimum, and KPRC News reporters and photographers sent back some of the most graphic descriptions and pictures ever made of a tropical hurricane.

On the team covering the massive storm was Tom Jarriel, then assistant news director of KPRC-TV, now Washington correspondent and weekend anchor for ABC. Tom was sent to Galveston, where he took an upper-floor room in the Buccaneer Hotel, overlooking the seawall and beachfront. The Buccaneer has since been converted into a retirement home operated by the United Methodist Church. Then, as now, the building offered a wide-angle view of Galveston's most famous landmarks including, at that time, Murdoch's bathhouse and pier, which had weathered more than fifty years of gulf storms, and the notorious Balinese Room, one-time showplace and gambling casino operated by the Maceo brothers.

As Tom watched through his camera viewfinder, the huge wind-driven waves smashed against the seawall, climbing higher and higher, until gushers of foam reached above utility poles and light standards along Seawall Boulevard. The boulevard itself began to fill with planking and timbers torn from the piers, huge scraps of sheet metal, and tattered remnants of signboards. Broken-winged seabirds struggled pitifully in the water that churned in the street.

One by one, familiar landmarks began to fall. A section of Murdoch's bathhouse collapsed, and the long pier connecting the Balinese Room to the promenade along the boulevard disappeared.

As the storm pushed inland, Galveston Island was swept by a line of tornadoes, spreading devastation through city streets, blocks from the waterfront. Whole buildings, many of them veterans of less violent gulf storms, were torn apart. Emergency shelters filled, and ambulances and rescue crews fought howling winds and driving rain. Tom went with them, recording on film the devastation and tragedy of one of nature's most spectacular upheavals.

Behind the island, Galveston Bay began to rise until its waters crept over wharves and into the streets of downtown Galveston. That presented a new problem. High water from storm tides effectively cut off approaches at both ends of the causeway connecting the island with the mainland, although the tall span of the bridge itself remained far above water. Workers could not get into Galveston, and those on the island who wanted to leave could not get out. Among them was Tom Jarriel. He had hundreds of feet of exciting hurricane footage, and his instinct drove him to try to get his film processed and broadcast.

Back at the station, news director Ray Miller and other managers were equally anxious to get Tom out. One suggestion was to charter a boat, brave the debris-filled waters of Galveston Bay, locate Tom, and bring him back. Perhaps with more confidence than he really felt, Miller said, "He'll get out." And Tom did, suddenly appearing at the station. He had waded through high water to reach the causeway, hitchhiked on a variety of emergency vehicles on the mainland, and finally thumbed a ride to Houston.

Tom was probably aware, and the rest of us certainly were, that any high ground near a flooded area was likely to be crawling with rattlesnakes, water moccasins, copperheads, and animals driven from their normal haunts by rising tides. If Tom knew it, he didn't let it stop him. The film he brought was spectacular, as we thought it would be. Even in black and white, the only thing available at the time, it still has the power today to keep a viewer transfixed.

With Tom's film, and other footage taken farther down the coast, we put together a documentary which, nearly thirty years later, is still used by the United States Weather Bureau for training purposes and for public instruction.

There is one ironic addition to this story. While Tom Jarriel was covering the storm from the Galveston beachfront, Dan Rather, then KHOU-TV's principal anchor, was reporting to his station and its viewers from the Weather Bureau in downtown Galveston. Stories about Rather's coverage during Carla reached New York and encouraged CBS to invite him to join that network's news staff. ABC, obviously impressed with Tom Jarriel in this assignment and in general, offered him a job.

Carla was by no means the last major hurricane KPRC-TV faced at close range. Among the more recent was "Alicia," which ravaged both Galveston and Houston in August 1983. In an article appearing shortly afterward in the technical journal, *Broadcast Engineering*, Ed Schafer, then engineering supervisor for Channel 2 News, gave the following account:

> . . . [Our] plans were put into effect on August 16, when [the] hurricane began to pose a threat to the upper Gulf Coast. Tracking was done through weather bureau information, satellite pictures, weather radar called up along the coast from Florida to Mexico, and our radar when the hurricane came within its range.
>
> KPRC-TV was well prepared when it became obvious that [this] immediate area was the site of the impending landfall. A

land unit was sent to Galveston and began feeding reports from locations along the seawall on the Gulf. As wind velocity increased, this unit moved to the Galveston post office building, which housed the weather bureau. Editing facilities were set up along with a microwave link to KPRC-TV's Houston repeater. The other live units were dispatched to other coastal areas within the range of our two repeaters.

On August 18, when Hurricane Alicia moved inland, the planning began to pay off. At no time did our station lose any of its microwave signals. We were able to go live from protected areas and from the Galveston weather bureau. KPRC continued full coverage with only minor electrical power kicks. So successful was the operation of our remote location in Galveston, along with our own news feeds, that NBC and CBS asked for feeds from there also. At our studio, we had sufficient editing facilities to allow other stations to edit packages for outgoing transmissions not only into Texas, but also as far away as the BBC.

As expected, there were problems. All were minor, with one exception. The live unit in Galveston was parked on the sheltered side of the post office building. In spite of this, five windows were lost as a result of wind pressure. All equipment in the vehicle, except the microwave gear, was ruined because of exposure to high-salt-content water. The loss amounted to approximately $70,000, but no staff members were injured.

As the United States space program gained momentum and the Manned Spacecraft Center at Clear Lake became the heart of its operations, KPRC-TV became a vital link in transmitting to the nation and the world the story of this assault on man's last frontier. Channel 2 News devoted time, equipment, and personnel to this fascinating story. And as Houston's explosive growth increasingly captured the attention and imagination of the rest of the country, Channel 2 was frequently called upon to provide coverage of major stories to the NBC network.

Not all those reports were pretty. One of the ugliest was that of the mass murders of more than two dozen young men. Another was a confrontation in Moody Park which became a riot. KPRC-TV reporters brought these events, and thousands more, to a growing viewer audience.

As news operations grew more sophisticated and complex, it became evident a joint news department, serving both television and radio, no longer provided the best answer for either. The two news organizations were fully separated. Ray Miller had built the TV news staff and chose to stay with that side of the operation.

Over the years, KPRC-TV News has earned most of the major awards available to local stations, including probably the most prestigious of all, the George Foster Peabody Award, presented in 1972 for a documentary, "The Right Man." Gary James, who wrote, photographed, and produced the program, still produces the classic "The Eyes of Texas" for KPRC-TV and stations throughout the state.

KPRC-TV News has provided more than its share of professionals who have gone on to network and other top assignments. Among them are Tom Jarriel, Chris Bury, and Chuck Pharris of ABC; Larry Weidman, Roger O'Neill, Dan Molina, Mauri Moore, and Velma Cato of NBC. Kay Bailey, Houston's first woman television reporter, later served as state representative, then as a member of the National Transportation Safety Board. Frank Dobbs became a motion picture director and producer. Bill Sprague joined the staff of Voice of America. A number of foreign news broadcasters also interned here, including one or more from Australia, Belgium, Turkey, the Philippines, Japan, Yugoslavia, Nigeria, and Great Britain. Alasdair Milne, one of our English interns, became director general of the British Broadcasting Company.

Besides its day-to-day coverage of events in Houston and the Southwest and its handling of dozens of assignments for NBC, Channel 2 News has also produced a long list of superior documentaries. Specials such as "Guns are for Killing," "61 Reisner Street," "In the Midst of Plenty," and "Tell It Like It Is" were scheduled on a semi-regular basis.

Many of these programs won significant awards, but even more important is the fact that the station produced them and played them in prime time, believing they were of sufficient value to the community to displace popular network entertainment programs.

With the advent of satellite capability, Channel 2 News became one of the first in the country to use this new opportunity to expand its field operation beyond the physical horizon. KPRC-TV acquired its own satellite mobile unit and became a founding member of the CONUS group, an association of similarly equipped news departments, each capable of originating on-the-spot coverage of breaking stories almost anywhere in the country, and exchanging such reports with other members of the group.

Channel 2 News will not pause to enjoy its accomplishments. It was established by groundbreakers in news broadcasting and it has pushed steadily ahead at the forefront of new developments in practices, techniques, and equipment. And under the leadership of its current director, Paul Paolicelli, who has almost a quarter-century of broadcast news experience, it will continue to be numbered among that relative handful of news organizations which are simply, but most accurately, described as "the best in the business."

A Few Good Men

FRANK Q. DOBBS

A few good men — that's a pretty accurate description of KPRC News in the 1960s, a time when television news on both the network and local level was beginning to come into its own.

John Cameron Swayze had given way to Huntley-Brinkley in New York and Washington for NBC. The new team was experienced at news gathering as well as news reading. And when Walter Cronkite, another former correspondent and one-time Houston newspaper reporter, was added as anchorman at CBS, network television news became serious business.

At Channel 2, news was already serious business, but early television technology limited coverage. Pictures of anything more than the anchorman's stern visage were infrequent, and even those rare occurrences usually consisted of sketches, Polaroid photographs, wire service photos, or, on special occasions, a bleary gray film shot of a reporter standing at or near the scene of a story, almost shouting into an ice-cream-cone-sized microphone connected to an old Auricon optical-sound newsreel camera.

As technology began to offer portable equipment, Channel 2 News took to the field. First, there was one station wagon. Then there were three and then four. By 1968, the news operation commanded a fleet of big-engined Ford Mustangs, able to keep up with just about any pursuit, and often called on to do just that.

Slowly, during the sixties, a time when Ray Miller ran the department — and the assignments desk, and the film editing room, and worked twelve- to fourteen-hour days — the concept of street reporting teams began to take shape. The call went out for additional manpower. Like the Marine Corps, KPRC News wanted a few good men; some experience necessary, but not as required as was a willingness for long hours and an ambition to achieve excellence.

I went to work for Channel 2 News in October 1964. For experience, I could claim three months as a small-town newspaper reporter *(The Conroe Daily Courier)* and eleven months as the only newsman at KBTX-TV in Bryan-College Station. My ambition was to make films, any and every kind of film, and Miller was pointing KPRC-TV News in that direction. Since filmmaking was so new to local television news, I quickly discovered I knew just about as much as anyone else. What I didn't know was the ins and outs of news reporting in a big city.

Tradition had it that the new man went to work on the police beat. This custom has since changed, and for the better, but at 6:00 A.M. on a chilly Monday morning in October, I picked up an old springwound Bell and Howell 16-millimeter film camera, a shoebox full of unexposed film, and a set of station wagon keys. I drove to 61 Reisner Street, Houston's downtown police station, ready for anything — I thought.

In those days, the police reporter provided newsfilm for KPRC-TV's early and late evening newscasts, and also fed voice reports to KPRC Radio for the hourly news broadcasts. So the equipment in the wagon I was driving included a two-way shortwave transmitter-receiver and a scanner tuned to police and fire department radio bands. As daylight began to break over Houston's skyline, the scanner came alive with the bells of a multiple-alarm fire. It was my first big story!

I roared down Fannin Street, steering with one hand and loading the camera on the seat beside me with the other. I drove until a tangle of fire hoses and a police officer blocked my path, then I jumped out and ran through thick smoke until I saw flames. I oriented myself by street signs, then rushed back to my station wagon to call in a live, direct-from-the-scene bulletin.

I managed to control my gasping breath and my pounding pulse and announced that smoke and flames were at that moment engulfing a major furniture store. Then I rushed back to the fire and discovered that it wasn't the furniture store at all; the fire was in an abandoned building next door, and the store wasn't in any

real danger. The walk back to the station wagon was like a con-
demned criminal's "last mile." Over the two-way, I confessed my
error, in effect admitting my failure in the news business.

As luck would have it, my luck that is, the early morning news
desk at the station on Post Oak was being managed by Tommy Jarriel, then our assistant news director. I expected blistering invective
and, at the very least, immediate dismissal. Instead, Tommy took
my confession calmly, dictated the basic format of a retraction I
was to record for the next radio news broadcast, and told me to
hurry back to the fire and get some good pictures for television.

Even so, I fully expected to be told when I returned to the station to turn in my press pass, my camera and car keys, and to look
for another job. But, to this day, more than twenty years later, I
have never been reminded of my folly. I suspect the genuine quaver
in my voice as I delivered my retraction on the 8:00 A.M. radio
news, allied with Tommy's patient understanding, were enough to
save my job.

Or it could have been the big scoop that I had. I got the credit,
but the idea should be credited to Will Sinclair. I was the early AM
outside man. Will handled the morning drive time "on-the-air"
radio newscasts. For several days the city had been in suspense
about the appointment of a new police chief. Then Mayor Louie
Welch was being very cagey with the news media, but he did schedule a noon hour press conference for an unorthodox Friday. Will
called me at the police station press room and suggested I telephone the homes of the three most prominent candidates for the
job, then offer my congratulations to whomever answered the call.

I did as I was told. The first answer was a little confused. The
second answer was, "But that isn't supposed to be announced until
noon." That's how cub reporter Frank Dobbs was able to break the
news that Herman Short would become Houston's next chief of police. No other station was willing to even report the rumor until the
noon press conference and Mayor Welch's confirmation of the
KPRC News scoop.

Unfortunately, not all those moments of inspiration work out
so well. Larry Rasco, Channel 2's anchor for the 6:00 and 10:00
P.M. newscast during the sixties and early seventies, got a call
one night from a family friend who was a nurse at one of the city's
major hospitals. She reported that Judge Roy Hofheinz, former
county judge, mayor, and guiding genius behind the Astrodome

complex, had just been brought in as an emergency case. Larry immediately called the hospital and the judge's wife, Mary Frances, was put on the telephone. She assured Larry in a very warm and calm voice that the judge was just in for a check-up but had gone downstairs for a cup of coffee. She asked if she should have Judge Hofheinz call when he returned to the room. Larry told her not to bother and apologized for any inconvenience.

The next morning, after the judge's family and business associates had performed the necessary "damage control," an official news announcement was made. Judge Hofheinz had suffered a massive stroke from which he would never fully recover. Mary Frances Hofheinz, an example of grace under pressure, had faked the news veteran right out of his shoes.

Special programs have always been a hallmark of Houston's KPRC-TV. When I signed on with Channel 2, a project called "Guns are for Killing" was already in the works. Miller was doing the narrating and producing, Chuck Pharris and Bob Harper were handling the cameras, and Bob Marich was directing a telling survey of the tragic consequences of easy access to handguns. I offered to carry gear, set up the lights, and monitor the sound recording.

The project was prompted by the assassination of President John F. Kennedy, killed by a sniper using an almost antique mail-order rifle. The report was very graphic, making extensive use of film from police homicide cases and the carnage of accidental shootings. But another disturbing segment concentrated on a fourteen-year-old Houston youngster who simply clipped a coupon from an outdoor magazine and forwarded it, along with a money order, to a Chicago address. By return mail, with no questions asked, he received a .45-caliber British military surplus revolver, in full and deadly working order.

"Guns are for Killing" created awareness of the problem and provoked a violent reaction directed principally at Miller, whose home was attacked on several occasions. But it won national awards and played a major role in getting laws passed restricting sales of firearms through the mail.

It also set another high standard for KPRC-TV News. Jack Harris, the station's general manager, brought the heads of the news and sales departments together and committed the station to produce an ongoing series of public service documentary programs. The charge to the news group was to develop such shows on a regular basis. Sales was to find sponsors willing to underwrite regularly scheduled public service documentaries. It was a radical concept for a local television station. Since I had already volunteered for the initial effort and hadn't worked myself into a position of critical responsibility in other phases of the news operation, I was assigned to help produce what would in time become a long series of award-winning television specials.

KPRC News was to create half-hour documentaries about Houston and Houstonians: who they were, what they did, their successes and failures. As we started to look closely at the project, a young Houston police officer was shot dead as he wrote a traffic ticket on a downtown street. That act of senseless violence helped focus our efforts.

Houston's police department was in a period of almost constant turmoil, and finding ways to recruit officers and hold them on the force was a continuing frustration. We called our program "61 Reisner Street," and it demonstrated why the old saying, "A policeman's lot is not a happy one," remains so apt. For nearly three weeks, chief news cameraman Bob Harper and I rode in the back of a police car, camera and sound gear in our laps.

We showed up at the scene of every conceivable type of police activity. And the truth that came through clearly was that most people resented the police and, as a result, officers turned increasingly inward. Eventually, the resentment seemed to run both ways. With the program's recognition of this problem, both the public and the department began to work to reduce resentment. That was more than twenty years ago. While this situation is not completely resolved, there is better understanding in the community, more manpower, and better morale on the force.

With some of Houston's problems it took more than one try at the subject. In the mid-1960s the city was wrapped up in a paradox over water. Lake Houston, Lake Conroe, and Lake Livingston were all holding millions of acre-feet of water, but Houston was still drawing from a dwindling underground water table through dozens of wells, and being throttled by a completely inadequate distribution system. Summer water shortages were a regular occurrence, but the shortages were at the faucet, not in the supply.

We put together an investigative report, "In the Midst of Plenty," opening with a scene showing Mayor Louie Welch reading an emergency ordinance declaring water rationing, then explaining why it was necessary.

Unfortunately, the program was less than fully effective. Eight years later, in the midst of yet another water crisis, we remade the program and began exactly the same way, with the earlier recitation by Mayor Welch. That was the year Houston finally began to deal with its inadequate distribution system.

Another show about civic responsibility got much higher marks for success and was nominated for an Emmy Award. "Tell It Like It Is" was a tour of an area of abject poverty, a classic slum without running water or sewage service, just five blocks north of downtown Houston. The area was populated by about 500 displaced blacks who called their decrepit neighborhood "the Bottoms — cause, man, you can't get no lower than this."

We needed no narration track on "Tell It Like It Is." We let the people of the Bottoms, some apathetic, some enraged, some trusting in a better life to come, tell their own stories and they let us film their daily lives. In the shadows of gleaming skyscrapers, these citizens carried water in buckets and dug latrines in their backyards.

Within a year, the Bottoms was no more. Both the city and private enterprise moved in to fix up the repairable, knock down the abandoned ruins, pave streets, and install water lines and sewers. "Tell It Like It Is" evoked embarrassment to civic pride, and there were some complaints from overzealous civic boosters. We of Channel 2 News thought the response to the show spoke for us, and we were damn proud.

The results of our efforts weren't always so uplifting. In late 1966, American forces were becoming fully engaged in Vietnam. Ray Miller decided to put together a show about local men and women in the war zone. We named it "A Christmas Card from Vietnam." The idea was to solicit names and locations of Houston area residents who were in South Vietnam and bring back filmed messages to the home folks. Miller asked me to make the trip with him, knowing I'd spent 1962 and 1963 as an army officer, and that my younger brother was serving as a pilot with a helicopter unit at Pleiku, in the central highlands of South Vietnam.

Miller and I spent the month of December 1966, traveling throughout Vietnam in every type of transportation, meeting men and women who came from the Houston area. We put together not one, but two documentaries, and I managed to spend a few days with my brother.

Each weekend we would collect our exposed film, hitch a ride into Saigon, and ship the film back to Houston, where Gary James was responsible for sorting it to build a series of reports from the combat zone about the country, the people, and the fighting. He also edited together all the Christmas messages from Texans at war.

The Christmas show was a big success. And when Miller and I returned to Houston, we worked with Gary to assemble a one-hour compilation of our reports. This documentary was called "Vietnam Diary," and it went on the air at a time when there was a long lull in the fighting. American forces were having trouble even finding the enemy, much less provoking combat. The war appeared to be winding down, and that was the summation of our program. Then came the Tet Offensive and a whole new perspective for all of us.

Bill Broyles, a former *Newsweek* and *Texas Monthly* editor, and a one-time Houstonian, wrote an article for *Esquire* called "Why Men Love War." From my own brief experiences I found the article frighteningly accurate. The survivors retain memories, both good and bad, that are forever denied to others.

My own special memory is of a chance meeting with famed author John Steinbeck on a trail deep in the Vietnam jungle. He was touring with a Marine Corps officer I had met earlier, so the Marine introduced us, as one journalist to another. Steinbeck wore a hearing aid in each ear but, even with that assistance, was almost completely deaf. The brief conversation was loud but cordial. We spoke about the rain and the lull in the battle. We shook hands, and he departed down the trail. Just as the two men rounded the bend, Steinbeck's voice rose again: "Frank Dobbs? Who the hell is he? Never heard of him!"

As the 1960s wound down, we were still producing documentary programs on a regular basis. I particularly remember one show that didn't get done, however. A potential sponsor came to the station with an idea for a show about pollution. He took the position that a little pollution wasn't necessarily a bad thing, that it was sometimes an unavoidable sign of progress and growth and should be accepted as such. Jack Harris and Ray Miller didn't buy.

We were quick to move on the early organ transplant activity at the Texas Medical Center, finishing a show called "The Pursuit of Immortality" within weeks of the first successful Houston heart transplants. But Miller didn't want a program that was only about heart transplants — everybody would be doing that one, he said. Instead, he wanted to examine the whole concept of organ transplants. So we covered the eye banks and cornea transplants and bone marrow transfers and kidney exchanges, predicting with remarkable accuracy the potential for such medical marvels. We had no idea, of course, how fast and furious the pace of such futuristic developments would become.

Governor John Connally pushed the idea of Texas tourism as an industry through the state legislature, creating the Texas Tourist Trails. This led us to a half-hour film tour of the ten designated trails, which pretty well covered the state. "More Than a State of Mind" was even narrated by the governor himself. Connally was at first reluctant to get so involved, but Mrs. Oveta Culp Hobby placed a personal call, reasoned with him about the opportunity, and he made time in his schedule to record the narration.

In the process of putting that show together, Miller became even more aware of just how much of our Texas heritage, both historic and geographic, was becoming lost due to thoughtless development or neglect. The result of his concern was an assignment to produce a documentary program which took its title from a sixteenth-century Spanish soldier of fortune's graphic story of the purposeful destruction of the Aztec empire of Central Mexico. To sum up his lengthy narrative, Bernal Diaz wrote: "Of all these wonders that I then beheld, all is overthrown and lost."

Again Miller, Gary James, and I toured Texas, and our program, "Of All These Wonders," created great interest in the preservation of historic places. It led, somewhat indirectly, to one of the most successful and long-running achievements for any local television station in the United States. Jack Harris liked the show and asked Miller about the possibility of doing a program on the same general subject more frequently — like maybe once a week.

In the early days of Texas television, Humble Oil and Refining Company had sponsored a program called "Texas in Review," made up of black-and-white film clips from sources all over the state. As Humble was absorbed into its parent company and successively became ESSO, ENCO, and EXXON, focus was directed to national markets, so the series was dropped.

What Harris and Miller had in mind was more elaborate and would not rely on outside sources for film clips. Instead, we would originate our own stories and put them together in a format using the most modern production techniques. The program, of course, was "The Eyes of Texas," and Gary James was the other original staffer for the project.

While I continued to work on "The Eyes of Texas" from time to time, I also produced the six-o'clock news on a daily basis and was assigned to other documentary programs. Management at KPRC-TV encouraged the submission of ideas from every level of the company. I frequently took advantage of this system, bombarding Miller and anyone else who would listen with story ideas and topics.

One such notion, which became a genuine coup, resulted from a conversation overheard in an elevator in the EXXON building in downtown Houston. While riding down forty-two floors from the Petroleum Club to the lobby, I heard an EXXON publications editor and another EXXON executive discussing Prudhoe Bay, a new oil and gas field being developed in Alaska, and a project they referred to as the "Ice Breaker Test."

I passed the tip to Miller, who suggested I contact EXXON with a direct inquiry. But EXXON wasn't ready to provide an answer. They were not prepared to make any announcement at all. In fact, EXXON was on the spot.

The newsman's instinct in such a situation is to get the story, and Miller followed his instinct. He cut a deal with EXXON's public affairs section. We would not go public with what we knew or could guess, and if and when EXXON went forward with the project we would be assured of an exclusive opportunity to cover the story. And that's why, when EXXON and British Petroleum finally announced a joint venture to send a huge ice-breaking oil tanker through the legendary Northwest Passage from east to west and back again, to explore the possibility of transporting by water Alaskan crude oil to East Coast and European markets, we were the only television organization, local or network, permitted to sign on for the entire voyage.

Since I provided the initial information, I was given the opportunity to make the trip as cameraman. Miller nominated himself as reporter. All three networks showed the SS *Manhattan*'s departure from New York in late August 1969, and CBS was even allowed to put a camera team on board for a part of the westward voyage, but only Channel 2 News, Houston, covered the passage through the icebound Arctic Ocean, first to last, and documented the consignment of the first load of Prudhoe Bay golden crude.

The result was both a documentary and an adventure. In many ways, "Passage to Prudhoe" was a forerunner of the series of films made later by Jacques Cousteau, as he sailed the world's oceans in his research vessel *Calypso*.

The *Manhattan* was under instructions to find the thickest ice shelf in the high Arctic and deliberately get stuck in the twenty-foot-thick pressure floes. After sitting immobile in ice for nearly two days, the ship's captain called for full power to free the 900-foot ship from nature's trap. There was serious concern as to whether the vessel could break free. If not, we were destined to spend the winter icebound.

That all-out effort to break the ice became the natural climax of our film. In quick succession came the orders: "All ahead full! Full astern!" Then again, "All ahead full!" The huge ship surged back and forth, each time crushing a little more of the ice wall which surrounded her. Suddenly, the *Manhattan* was moving ahead — only three days from Prudhoe Bay. That combination of dramatic confrontation and cliff-hanging suspense, in a completely real situation, made an almost perfect television subject.

Three days later, as the ice-breaking *Manhattan* dropped anchor off a Canadian Eskimo village so that a group of dignitaries could be ferried out to the vessel, Ray Miller "sneaked" aboard the helicopter for the return trip. He showed up in Seattle at the NBC affiliate early the next morning, and "The Nightly News" with Huntley and Brinkley offered first film of the "cliff-hanging" test to a nationwide audience. The show's final credits gave the nod to KPRC-TV in Houston for the report from the high Arctic.

"Passage to Prudhoe" won several awards, and EXXON ordered dozens of copies of the completed program to be shown to employees, customers, and suppliers around the world.

In spite of its long list of distinguished documentary programs, the principal concern of Channel 2 News is, as it has always been, today's news. Being a part of a documentary crew was and is an opportunity in addition to regular news-gathering duties. While my morning might be spent doing an interview for an upcoming proj-

ect, my afternoon was devoted to gathering and editing at least one
story for the evening news.

In the bizarre incident which was later dramatized in Steven
Spielberg's film, "Sugarland Express," the entire staff of Channel 2
News was put to work covering a story from the ground and from
the air as it unfolded, hour by hour, mile by mile.

Miller called me in from editing a documentary to collect field
reports and write bulletins as a caravan of police vehicles wound its
way across Texas, following a commandeered state highway patrol
car driven by the hostage officer. Jack Cato, already recognized as
one of the best police reporters in the country, was five cars behind
the fugitive vehicle. Gary James left his "Eyes of Texas" desk and
made his first flight in the brand new Bell Jet Ranger helicopter to
provide aerial coverage of the chase. One way or another, every
member of the news staff took part as that long afternoon pro-
gressed to the final confrontation at a farmhouse near College Station.

The 1988 story from Midland of the little girl trapped in an
abandoned well reminded me of a similar incident nearer home and
almost exactly twenty years earlier. I was called away from a late-
night party and assigned to meet reporter Steve Smith at a farmhouse near the Big Thicket community of Votaw. A young couple
had called for help after their two-year-old daughter had acciden-
tally fallen into a clay pipe-lined well and was wedged tightly in a
bend in the pipe about twenty-five feet below the surface.

Construction crews from Brown and Root were called on to
provide a giant foundation-drilling machine, and volunteer rescue
squads from all over East Texas converged on the small community. A late-night rescue operation got under way.

Satellites and live video trucks were only science fiction
dreams in those days, so a nationwide audience stood by their radios, listening to constant updates and waiting anxiously for film
reports which were promised to follow. Just before dawn, a Houston volunteer, Ransom Bill, broke through the pipe with a sledge-
hammer, grabbed the little girl by the arms, and yelled to be pulled
to the surface. In the tight close-up view from my camera, two
heads popped out of the excavation, cheek to cheek: Bill with a big
grin on his dirty face, and the teary-eyed two-year-old crying for
her mama. We strained the speed limit driving back to the studios,
where lab manager Chuck White had the film processor warmed

and waiting. The first pictures of the frantic rescue effort and its triumphant conclusion were ready just in time for the early-morning network news, direct from KPRC-TV, Houston.

That was and is what television news is all about. Every member of the Channel 2 News staff, past and present, has memories like these — memories of challenges met and obstacles overcome, of digging into the story and getting it told. Today the roll call of the newsroom takes a good deal longer, to match the widely expanded area its people cover and the variety and complexity of the facilities they use. And it now includes more than a few good women.

Those of us classified as old-timers now sit and watch, listening and marveling, as our successors exhibit their skills, their dedication, and their professionalism. When we get together to reminisce about "old times," we like to claim today's newspeople as worthy heirs of the standards we set, when a news camera was powered by a tension spring, if we remembered to wind it, and voice reports were called in from a pay phone, if we had a dime.

An Episode in Moody Park

PHIL ARCHER AND JACK CATO

In May 1978, Jack Cato and Phil Archer were the Channel 2 News dayside and nightside police reporters, but they often worked together. Houston's Moody Park lies between White Oak Bayou and Fulton Street, a few blocks east of IH-45, in an area which has become an inner-city barrio. The story of the evening of Sunday, May 8, is told, alternately, by Archer and Cato.

Archer: On Sundays my shift ran from 6:00 P.M. to 2:00 A.M. As soon as I started that evening, I picked up a stabbing death somewhere on the northeast side of town. Jack Cato met me there. Jack wasn't on duty, but he often rode with me just for the fun of it. He was driving a Dodge Charger, his new station news car. He'd just had all the police radios installed, and as soon as I finished taping, I transferred my gear to Jack's car.

Cato: Cruising and looking and listening to the police radio is common for police reporters. There was a call from an ambulance supervisor, asking for help at Moody Park, at the corner of Fulton and Collingsworth.

Archer: We got a little information from the police dispatcher over Jack's car phone, but the dispatcher didn't know much more than we did. We couldn't raise anyone back at the station on the phone or the two-way radio. Sara Lowery, the weekend anchor, was the only one in the newsroom at that time Sunday evening, and was probably upstairs taping the network news feed.

Cato: We took the Patton Street exit off the freeway, and when we turned at Fulton there were six police cars blocking the street. I parked on the sidewalk in front of a funeral home. Phil had a tape camera, so we took that and I left my film camera in the car.

As we started walking south on Fulton, two police officers were coming out of the park. One was leading a prisoner and the other had blood on his face. Two blocks away, just inside the park, we could see a burning car. An officer told us a man had been stabbed in a fight inside the park, and when the ambulance arrived, there was a confrontation. The fire department paramedic and the injured man had to battle their way out. The ambulance supervisor abandoned his car and rode out with them, and the mob turned his car over and set it on fire.

Archer: We could see a crowd of people milling around in the park, but couldn't make out how many because trees blocked our view. I could hear a woman's voice talking to them over a public address system in both English and Spanish, but couldn't tell what she was saying. There were also groups gathered along the street and a steady stream of bricks, rocks, and bottles was coming from that direction aimed at the police cars. I don't think I'll ever forget the sound a brick makes when it ricochets off a car hood.

Jack was anxious to get up close to the burning car to tape it before the fire went out. The police warned it would be dangerous to go beyond the line they had set up, but neither of us was especially concerned about getting hurt. We were excited about being the only newsmen on the scene of a major breaking story, and had been in similar situations covering police stories, following cops into hostile neighborhoods. It was usually police, not reporters, who were objects of hostility.

Cato: As we walked toward the burning car, the PA speaker was rambling about how bad the Houston Police Department was, and that the people needed to show their hate for the treatment they had been given. Just about a block before we reached the car, a crowd of young Mexican-Americans surrounded us.

Archer: I guess the oldest was about fifteen. This wasn't unusual in inner-city neighborhoods. Just about any time a reporter showed up on a police scene, kids would jump in front of the camera, trying to get on TV. There were no threats or open hostilities. In fact, the mood of the crowd around us was almost festive.

But then a second group showed up. They came from the direction of the park and were older, somewhere in the eighteen- to twenty-year range. I remember looking at one kid as he ran up to us, thinking his eyes looked strange, like he might have been high on something.

I was still taping and Jack was talking to the crowd, trying to make friends. Then someone picked up a bicycle and threw it at us. I was concentrating on the viewfinder and didn't see it coming. It hit me on the camera side and jostled my shot.

Cato: Then came rocks. One hit me in the face, and Phil and I knew we had to get out of there. As I turned, three youths jumped Phil. I yelled, "Get off him!" and turned to pick up the camera and recorder Phil had dropped when he was jumped. I looked around in time to see a young Mexican-American running toward me. I turned to run but it was too late. I felt the rush of blood on my back and knew I had been stabbed.

My first thought was: you die when you're stabbed in the back. Will I bleed to death before I can get out? But then the crowd of youngsters came to my rescue. "Can we help?" they asked, and offered to carry my equipment. It was a long two blocks. I could hardly see through blood running into my eyes from the cuts that rocks had made in my forehead. Then a paramedic grabbed my arm and led me into the ambulance.

Archer: When we began to run back toward the police line, the crowd was right behind us. Someone grabbed the cable from my camera to the battery belt and yanked. I turned and saw one of the young men jumping up and down on my camera. To a photographer that's like seeing someone beating one of your kids. I remember yelling, "Don't do that! That camera's expensive!" Then a brick came flying out of the crowd and hit me between the eyes. That's the only time in my life I actually saw stars.

I passed out. When I came to, a couple of kids were dragging me to the police line. I tried to walk, but my left leg wouldn't hold me. Two or three officers came to help. There were about twenty officers now, and most were guys I knew from working the police beat. I guess my appearance worried them. My face looked like hamburger, with cuts and bruises and a particularly nasty gash on the top of my head.

Worst of all, I'd been stabbed in the lower left buttock, and the cops were afraid I was going to bleed to death before they could get me out. I was wearing a pair of light blue pants that day, but you couldn't tell it. They were completely soaked with blood.

The officers thought I had been stabbed in the crotch, so they laid me on the hood of a patrol car. A female officer who had been a nurse ripped open my pants and began checking to see if I'd been castrated. About that time a cameraman from the ABC station showed up and began taping. His tape played on all the networks. My first network exposure was very compromising!

I was dazed and confused but didn't feel any pain because I was in shock. I kept floating in and out of consciousness, embarrassed about the fuss the cops were making over me. I worried about Jack. I thought he might still be back in the street. Then they told me he had been taken out in an ambulance.

I was really worried when I realized my camera was missing. There's a saying in our shop that if you don't come back with your camera, you might as well not come back. I tried to get up to look for it, but the cops wouldn't let me.

It was like Fort Apache. The little group of police cars was a small island in the middle of a riot. Rocks and bottles were raining down on us, and everyone was pretty worked up.

Then it dawned on me that with both of us out of action, Channel 2 didn't have anyone covering the story. There were no other news crews working that Sunday and most of the regular staff was on the way back from Austin, where they had been assigned to the state primaries. I started to get up to call Ray Miller at home, but a cop pushed me back down on the car hood.

They were having a problem getting an ambulance through the crowd to pick me up. Finally, they put me in the back seat of a patrol car and drove me out. I remember hearing bricks and bottles bouncing off the car. They told me later that one of the bricks smashed the windshield. Outside the park, they transferred me to an ambulance and took me to Northwest Memorial Hospital.

Jack was already there, in the emergency room, giving an interview to Steve Long while they were patching the hole in his back. Later that evening we sat in our hospital beds, watching Channel 2's coverage of the rioting as it continued into the night. I thought Jack was going to cry when the shot of his station news car came on the screen. It was flipped on its top, burning like a torch in the middle of Fulton Street.

It took about a hundred stitches to close the cuts on my head.

The stab wound in my hip was two inches wide and just about as deep. I'd lost a lot of blood and the knife nicked the sciatic nerve, the main nerve trunk that runs down the leg. The doctor said if the wound had been a quarter-inch wider, it would have severed the nerve and crippled me for life. As it is, the back of my left thigh is permanently numb from buttocks to the knee, but I can still use my leg.

My memory of Moody Park is little more than a blur. Jack and I were in the park only about ten minutes before we were hurt, and I never saw who attacked me. But almost ten years later I got a better idea of what happened from Kenny Boles, who had been one of our reporters covering the story. He had talked with some of the cops who were in the police cars when Jack and I were attacked.

After Jack managed to stagger back to the police line, I was still out cold in the middle of the street. The cops claim the guy who stabbed me was standing over me with his knife, ready to finish the job, when a couple of kids in the crowd confronted him and told him that was enough. The guy backed off. I owe my life to those kids, and I think they're the same ones who dragged me to the police line.

(Editor's note: Station management, after some effort, was able to establish the identity of the two boys. Their parents, however, were reluctant for them to accept any reward, fearing reprisals in the community. Eventually, they agreed to let the station reward them, but it was done circumspectly, with absolutely no publicity.)

Archer: Jack and I spent a week in the hospital, and took another fourteen weeks to fully recover. My camera was returned to the station a couple of days after the riot. Someone found it in the street, with the lens broken off and the frame bent into a bow like the rocker of a chair. It was covered with blood and looked like it had been run over by a truck. Channel 2 engineers were astonished when they flipped the switch. The camera ran! I'm not sure how they wrote it off on the insurance claim.

Cato: When they showed me pictures of the people arrested during the riot, I recognized the man who stabbed me. That fall, when he was tried, he was sentenced to five years' probation. In the summer of 1987, nine years after the riot, he died of a drug overdose.

"Mama, I've Killed Dean!"

JACK CATO

The first report, midmorning, on Wednesday, August 8, 1973, was routine enough. A police dispatcher said a man had been killed in Pasadena, but that it was just a "queer" mess and to forget about it. I recognized the expression, even though it was not one used in polite conversation, but the dispatcher said to forget it, so I forgot it.

Then, about 3:30 in the afternoon, I got a tip that there was more to the killing. A suspect and several police officers were on their way to a place where the prisoner said several bodies were buried. The address was on Silver Bell Street, in far southwest Houston, between South Post Oak and Hiram Clark Road.

When I got there, the location turned out to be a boat shed on a quiet dead-end street. Three police detectives and a squad of trusties from the city jail were accompanied by a young man they identified as Elmer Wayne Henley. One of the detectives, Pasadena officer David Mullican, told me Henley had offered to show them where bodies had been buried under the shed. He gave me the okay to talk to Henley. Reporter Ann James held the tape recorder while I talked to the very tense young suspect. He would talk to us, but he would not let us photograph him, saying that he would talk "off camera" if he could use a telephone to call his mother. There was no phone in the shed and apparently none anywhere nearby.

The trusties, already at work, had uncovered one body. It was nearly 6:00 P.M., so I called into the station on the news car telephone, giving them an update. A couple of minutes after 6:00 they put me on the air with a live report from the scene. Just as I signed off, I announced that a second body had been uncovered. That was the first word of a series of murders in Houston.

I took some 16mm film of the trusties at work, then told Henley he could use the news car telephone. I dialed the number for him.

As his mother answered, Henley blurted out, "Mama, Mama, I've killed Dean!" The speaker on the car phone picked up every word. We had it all on tape.

I got back to the station with my pictures and the recorded confession barely in time to make the 10:00 P.M. news, did my report live, then hurried back to the shed on Silver Bell. By that time the trusties had placed eight bodies of boys and young men in hearses, and they were still digging.

I also found out the "Dean" that Henley had confessed to killing was a man named Dean Corll. I moved in on the detective in charge of the scene, Lt. Breck Porter, with my camera rolling and my portable light glaring. I asked him what he thought of the situation.

Porter, an old-time Houston cop with experience dating back to the 1940s, pushed his Stetson back on his head, hitched at his silver buckled belt with the pistol holster on the right hip, and drawled, "If Dean Corll was responsible for all this," he waved his arms to take in the scene, "then he had to be some perverted clown!"

The news clip, along with Henley's confession to his mother on the Channel 2 News mobile telephone, made every network newscast the next day. Over a period of several days, Henley, along with David Brooks, another young suspect involved in the case, showed Houston area officers where a total of twenty-seven bodies were buried. Seventeen were found in the boat shed on Silver Bell. The others were unearthed up and down a stretch of isolated beach at High Island, between Galveston and Port Arthur, and in the East Texas Piney Woods.

All twenty-seven were either teenaged boys or very young men, and all appeared to have been sexually molested and tortured before being killed. From statements made by Henley and Brooks, it appeared Corll had been the ringleader of the trio, and that the gruesome serial murders had been going on for several months.

Henley and Brooks were tried and convicted of murder and

are now serving life sentences in the Texas Department of Corrections. But the complete story has never really been told, and the chances are it never will be. There are still unidentified bodies lying in the Harris County morgue, despite the best efforts of police officers around the country and dozens of anxious parents of missing boys and youths. Some investigators are convinced there are other bodies still buried; bodies that may never be found.

Every police reporter has covered news stories he would like to forget — that he tries to forget — and can't. This one is mine.

The Right Man

HOW WE CAME TO FIND DR. ROBERT HAYES

JACK HARRIS

The owners of the *Houston Post* always maintained the strongest possible community ties, so when the Hobby family got into broadcasting, that tradition, by design, was carried over, and is still the guiding principle for all of the company's broadcast outlets.

It has always been my strong belief that a great communications organization is much more than just a business enterprise. Each of our stations, from top management right on through the organization, has always sought to be an integral part of the community it is licensed to serve.

I was filling that role at a luncheon at the Houston Club in 1972 when Dr. Robert Hayes, president of Wiley College in Marshall, Texas, spoke about privately endowed black colleges in America.

The KPRC stations, both radio and television, had been involved in several racial integration projects during the late 1960s. I had been pleased with the progress toward integration and especially due to the fact that it had been accomplished largely without violence. I knew integration had also been proceeding successfully in the state's larger universities, and I was comfortable in the belief that blacks were being given opportunities for higher education.

Dr. Hayes knocked my assumptions into a cocked hat. He proved to be one of the most interesting and inspiring speakers I had ever encountered, but the picture he painted was troubling.

He asserted that from their background and early public education in a school system that had, until very recently, been completely segregated, many young blacks were unable to cope with conditions they found on large, mainly white campuses of our bigger state universities. They needed the nurturing that could be found only on the small campuses of black colleges, where administrators and faculty members understood the difficulties. They needed special counseling and encouragement. They needed a learning pace that wouldn't throw them so far behind their classmates that they would be convinced their quest for knowledge was hopeless.

There were only thirty-one of these colleges in the United States, and surprisingly enough, almost one-fourth were in Texas. Taken as a group, the thirty-one black colleges had only a fraction of the endowment or the budget or the physical resources of, for example, Harvard or The University of Texas.

Dr. Hayes told the luncheon guests how he had originally been sent to Wiley College to supervise the school's closing, but he just couldn't bring himself to carry out his instructions. He instead began to fight and scratch to keep it alive. In 1972, Wiley College was still fighting for its life and needed help from business and civic leaders.

I left the luncheon determined that KPRC-TV would help Dr. Hayes spread the word about Wiley College and the other thirty small black colleges; not just to the business leaders, but to the hundreds of thousands of East Texans in our viewing audience.

KPRC News had the talented manpower to get the job done. Special projects producer Gary James was given the assignment.

PRODUCING "THE RIGHT MAN"

GARY JAMES

The year 1972 was a good one for TV documentary producers and cameramen, and especially for me. I won a couple of awards, my bosses were pleased with my work, and I had just completed a show I thought would be my "masterpiece." It was called "Football Fever," and was a report on the extremes of behavior of normally "reasonable and considerate" Texans during the annual high school football season.

I don't know the process behind front-office decisions, but

suddenly Ray Miller told me to pack my cameras, pick up another photographer, John Denny, and hit the road for Marshall, up near Caddo Lake in deep East Texas. We were to spend the next three days on the campus of Wiley College. Our subject was to be the college and its longtime president, Dr. Robert Hayes.

One of the things that has always helped make KPRC-TV documentary programs different and, we think, better, is an open-minded approach to the subject. In this case, we knew in a general way what we wanted the program to accomplish. We didn't have any particular notion of how we would reach that goal.

Too many filmmakers and reporters tend to try to force their stories and their interview subjects into a preconceived pattern, often missing real opportunities because they don't take the time to explore the potential. Frequently, the results of this kind of programming seem canned or artificial, especially when they are what we call "people" stories. Our approach is that people don't have to be nice but they must seem natural. Then the story is real. In Dr. Robert Hayes, we found both nice and natural.

We went to Marshall for a story about small black colleges struggling mightily to remain in operation. We were there to film campus life, take a look at the commencement exercises, and produce a little good P.R. for Wiley College. We got all that, but we also discovered a great man who, quite naturally, came to dominate our story — a man who became the story.

Dr. Hayes was friendly, pleasant, soft-spoken, and more. In fact, the first time we saw him, he was walking up a flight of stairs to his second-floor office, humming an old hymn and wearing a dark gray suit, topped off by a straw gardening hat. He explained that he had just finished weeding his garden and that his garden was where he always did his heavy thinking.

We knew immediately that this was a very special man. He had an indefinable effect on people, relaxed and yet intense. Students followed him around the school as if he were the Pied Piper. We would later learn that he had the same sort of impact on all kinds of people, in gatherings large or small, as he traveled tirelessly around the state, trying to drum up supporters to help keep his school afloat.

By the time our first interview was completed, we knew this show would need no script. Dr. Hayes would narrate the program, telling the story in his own words and at his own pace. We didn't have to do any directing. We explained each objective as we went along, and he did the rest.

The biggest problem was keeping the kindly educator to ourselves long enough to complete each segment. Every place we set up our camera, we were interrupted by students who idolized Dr. Hayes. We found that he knew everybody by name — every student, every teacher, every maintenance man. On campus, Dr. Hayes could be found one minute pulling weeds, and the next, counseling a group of admiring students on the steps of the administration building. One day he would be in Houston soliciting funds for Wiley College (he was an absolute master at fund-raising); the next day, back on campus, reaching into his own pocket to help a student make ends meet.

Our developing documentary was no longer just about Wiley College. It became the story of the man who was the school's heart and soul. It was the saga of a young black who grew up in a Houston ghetto and wanted an education more than anything else in life; the story of a man who worked his way through Wiley College as a janitor, then, determined to help other young blacks reach the same goal, made education his career. It was the story of a school janitor who returned years later as school president, determined that his school would not die.

We called our documentary "The Right Man." It played on Channel 2 in Houston. It also played on stations all over the United States under the sponsorship of UNCF, the United Negro College Fund. UNCF honored "The Right Man" with a special award, and KPRC-TV also won the most prestigious of all television honors, the George Foster Peabody Award — not for "Football Fever," but for "The Right Man." I would like to be able to claim the plaque as a recognition of our expertise as filmmakers, but the program really succeeded because of its star, Dr. Robert Hayes, "The Right Man."

THE RIGHT IDEA

JACK HARRIS

With the tremendous response to "The Right Man," the United Negro College Fund came to KPRC-TV for some more help. The station had long been successful in raising money for a number of charities and worthy causes through a series of telethons, and I thought the same technique could be used to effectively promote the cause of small black colleges just as it had been helpful in the fight against blindness, cancer, muscular dystrophy, and other dread diseases.

We prepared a telethon plan for the Texas chapter of UNCF to take to the national headquarters. We outlined all the essentials: the need for corporate sponsors, the need to line up affiliate stations for the telethon network, the need for volunteer workers at all locations, and ways and means of recruiting top talent for the on-camera appeals.

The Texas chapter tried mightily to get the national United Negro College Fund organization to embrace the idea but without success. The state chapter officers then asked if Channel 2 would try the program as a local or Texas-based effort. We agreed, and for several years, KPRC-TV produced a UNCF telethon locally, then made tapes of the show available to stations all over the state.

Measured against many telethons, the UNCF appeals were moderately successful, but to local and state UNCF officials, the resulting donations were far beyond any amount they had previously been able to raise. Eventually, the national organization, noting the success in Texas, embraced the idea of the telethon. Today it is the principal fund-raiser, helping to keep an important part of America's educational system alive and in improving health.

It all started with a luncheon speech by Dr. Robert Hayes, truly "The Right Man."

"The Eyes of Texas"

GARY JAMES

It is the longest-running regularly scheduled television program in Houston, discounting newscasts, and the longest-running syndicated television show in Texas. There are two big reasons for the success of "The Eyes of Texas." I think I share the credit for one of them. The reasons: it is a good program, and for two decades it has enjoyed the full support of management, even when it cost more money than it brought in.

"The Eyes of Texas" began as something of a fluke in the summer of 1969. For a number of years, Frank Dobbs and I had been "the" special projects unit of Channel 2 News, responsible for producing several major documentaries for prime-time viewing each TV season. That summer we had been trying to sell management on a documentary detailing the rise of the Mafia in South Texas and northern Mexico.

Our boss, Ray Miller, expressed genuine concern for our personal safety if we took cameras off to the border for such an expose. Finally, he decided to table the idea, at least for a while. That decision left two fidgety newsmen without a special project for the summer, but Ray wasn't about to let us stay idle for long. We learned that Ray and Channel 2's general manager, Jack Harris, had been discussing the merits of putting together a weekly half-hour program, heavy with picture stories and in-depth treatment of Texas people and places.

We turned out to be ideal for the job. Frank could turn out good story ideas and narration scripts very quickly. I was itching to try some new ideas with my camera and with the film editing table just acquired by the station. We both loved to travel.

A third member was assigned to the team, although not on a full-time basis, since he also directed many of the station's newscasts and special programs and was in demand by all three networks to direct Houston originations of space stories and sporting events. We were lucky to get Jon Burkhart. He spent hours each week using his directing skills and ideas to help give the program a freshly polished, big-budget look.

We started work on the new show in July of 1969. The name, "The Eyes of Texas," was not borrowed from The University of Texas song. Those words had been a part of the station logo from its earliest years. Since it was a perfect fit for the concept we were developing, we decided to adopt it as our title. We were hoping that the Aggies of Texas A&M wouldn't automatically turn us off. The hope was justified. Through the years, Aggies have been the subject of many feature stories and have become some of the show's biggest fans.

Ray Miller was the show's executive producer and narrator, but the expanding television news department took most of his time. Frank and I would meet with Ray once a week to talk about story ideas and receive specific assignments. For the most part, we were on our own and on the road.

Originally, the summer replacement program was scheduled at 10:30 P.M., following the news on Sunday nights, but it wasn't long before the show's popularity, reflected by petitions from schoolteachers and parents, caused a schedule change. People wanted "The Eyes of Texas" to be on at a time when the whole family could watch. The show eventually found an agreeable slot at 6:30 P.M. on Saturdays, where it has been a fixture all these years.

"The Eyes of Texas" was a forerunner of what has become known as the "PM Magazine" format, but from the beginning it was and still is more flexible. In the years since 1969, "Eyes" has traveled about a million miles, talked with thousands of Texans, and captured the essence of Texas from the Gulf Coast to the mountains and deserts of the far west, from the Rio Grande Valley citrus groves to the endless horizon of the Panhandle.

In the mid-1970s, other stations around the state began to schedule the show. Today, no matter where you live in the Lone Star State, you are more than likely familiar with it. The show continues to evolve, and that evolution continues to generate audience interest. New faces and new equipment have led to new techniques. Instead of spring-wound Bell and Howell film cameras, we now use high-speed video cameras. That editing table, state-of-the-art back in 1969, has long since been retired. Today we edit at computer keyboards.

All of the people who have worked with the show over the years have their favorite stories. I remember the day I drove into the small community of Yorktown, south of Victoria. I had called ahead and arranged to meet the subject of our story at City Hall, but when I drove up, the entire block in front of City Hall was roped off. I drove on down the street, found a parking spot, and trudged back down the block — only to find that the street had been roped off to make room for all the big remote video trucks the local folks were expecting.

If the people of Yorktown were expecting a big crew and vanloads of equipment, then I decided I must be doing my job right, even if I was a "one-man-band."

Twenty years, hundreds of stories, and thousands of memories have passed as the faces have continued to change. Frank Dobbs moved on to produce and direct theatrical movies. Bob Brandon followed Frank onto the show, then became a freelance cameraman, handling network assignments out of Denver, Colorado. Larry Weidman, now NBC bureau chief in Rome, was replaced by John Denny, who later published his own small-town newspaper and served as news director for a Dallas radio station. Rick Hartley became chief spokesman for the Texas Department of Corrections, then went into real estate. Jon Burkhart, the other founding staffer, has retired to Maui, Hawaii. However, he still returns to the mainland on occasion to direct network specials.

Bill Springer came aboard ten years ago, and he and I have become the "graybeards" of the shop, literally and figuratively. Ron Stone took over as narrator several years back, bringing a small-town upbringing and big-city savvy to the show. Ron, who is one of the most popular local news anchors in the country, has further expanded our horizons. "The Eyes of Texas" is no longer a two-man operation. Regular contributors to the show now include Joe Campos, Leslie Seamon, Pat Schwab, and Ron Stone, Jr. These new faces have introduced their own ideas for style and content.

I am sometimes asked if I get tired of doing "The Eyes of

Texas" (I'll celebrate my twentieth anniversary on the show in 1990). My answer is always a firm no. "The Eyes of Texas" is the kind of program I spent years wanting to do, then got to do, and still want to do. "The Eyes of Texas" has survived because it works. It is a slice right out of life, with stories of unusual people and places in an unusual land that people often associate only with oil wells and John Wayne characters. It lives on because the people we meet are not the stereotypes. They live on as real people in a real but still fascinating world.

My greatest satisfaction came several years ago when I picked up a broadcasting trade journal and found a list of the top 100 syndicated television programs in the country. Among the top five was "The Eyes of Texas." That, neighbors, is satisfaction.

Keep watching!

The LBJ Documentary

JACK McGREW

In the late summer of 1963, with the '64 presidential election only fifteen months away, Washington's rumor mill was speculating that President John Kennedy might "dump" Lyndon Johnson in favor of some other vice-presidential candidate more palatable to certain elements in the administration. It was no secret that the Texan was not universally admired in inner councils of the White House, although Kennedy himself had given no public hint of displeasure. In fact, he'd made substantial efforts to defuse the gossip. Nevertheless, supporters of Vice-President Johnson took the possibility seriously and set about strengthening their man's position.

Among those supporters were two other Texans: Jack Brooks, congressman from Beaumont, and Jack Valenti, partner in a Houston advertising agency and longtime adviser to Albert Thomas, the veteran and extremely influential congressman from Houston. Brooks and Valenti suggested that a television documentary, showing Johnson in his most comfortable role, that of a strong, confident leader in his beloved Hill Country of Central Texas, might convince administration leaders, and especially the president, that the winning combination of 1960 should remain intact.

Valenti was well known to Houston media, having grown up within its advertising community, and was on particularly good terms with Jack Harris and other members of the *Houston Post/* KPRC/KPRC-TV organization. He had little trouble selling the idea to Harris, and details were quickly resolved. KPRC-TV would send a crew, headed by Ray Miller and Bob Marich, a most imaginative director, to the LBJ Ranch near Stonewall on the Pedernales River, west of Austin. They would tape enough material for at least a one-hour documentary, in which the vice-president would have an opportunity to discuss his philosophies and ambitions for the country. The program would show Johnson and his family in their favorite setting.

I pulled enough rank to get myself attached to the project as a supernumerary and observer, with no specific assignment. I had known Valenti a long time, and was well acquainted with J. C. "Jess" Kellam, manager of Johnson's television station in Austin, who would be at the ranch to advise the Johnson family. So there may have been some vague idea that my being there might come in handy.

It was decided to produce the program on tape, rather than on film, although tape was still relatively new and the equipment was by no means mobile under ordinary circumstances. The tape machine was a large upright RCA unit intended for studio use, removed from the station's tape/film area and mounted in a van, along with two equally cumbersome studio cameras. The mobile unit, with its self-contained control room, made up another segment. And, since "rolling shots" were anticipated, a portable generator to supply power to the tape machines, cameras, and control room was fitted onto a trailer and attached to the truck. The resulting caravan was unorthodox but impressive.

In the planned scenario, Ray Miller would drive one of the ranch's vehicles, an antique Model A touring car, across a low-water crossing of the Pedernales a few yards downstream from the ranch house, and meet Johnson, mounted on his favorite horse. Johnson would dismount and join Miller in the car, then drive to a spot near the house. Both would sit on benches under a tree and discuss Johnson's ideas and plans. Then they would walk to the house, where Mrs. Johnson would greet them. A tour of the house would follow, and the Johnson daughters would be introduced. It was made quite clear by the vice-president that two areas were off-limits to our cameras: the swimming pool beside the house and the airstrip behind it.

After a time-consuming technical delay while the vice-president, attired in his working clothes, khaki trousers, and open-neck khaki shirt, sat patiently on his horse, quietly discussing business with his foreman, shooting on the first scene got under way. The conversation under the tree went well and, as planned, Johnson and Miller walked to the door where Mrs. Johnson waited. At this point, it was necessary to stop action in order to move the cameras indoors. This took the better part of an hour while the vice-president and Mrs. Johnson went on with the work of running the ranch. When all was ready they reappeared, but this time Johnson was wearing a tie and jacket.

Director Marich courteously reminded Johnson that when last seen on camera, he had been in shirt sleeves, with no tie or jacket, and that viewers would be confused if he appeared to change clothes as he stepped through the door. Johnson answered with authority: "I always wear a jacket and tie in the house." There was a long pause while Marich and Miller contemplated the impasse, then Mrs. Johnson broke the deadlock. She suggested that she conduct the house tour and it would appear to viewers that Johnson had left Miller at the door. Everyone agreed, so the vice-president disappeared, perhaps somewhat relieved, while Mrs. Johnson took over. She did so graciously and with considerable aplomb. Despite frequent interruptions to shift equipment from room to room, only one scene was done over, and that was due to a technical problem.

Freed from the production and with nothing on his schedule, Johnson decided to fly to Austin to get a haircut by his favorite barber at the Driskill Hotel. The twin-engine plane he used to commute back and forth between the ranch and one or the other of Austin's airfields taxied to the end of the runway, and as Marich watched, he decided to gamble. He instructed the crew to set up a camera beside the control room truck, where it would not be easily seen, and to be prepared to photograph the vice-president's return. Reminded that the airstrip was off-limits, Marich shrugged: "He'll never notice." Marich was wrong.

An hour or so later the plane reappeared and landed, and those watching the monitor in the control room saw the vice-president step into the driver's seat of the white golf cart he used to move around the area near the house. As the golf cart drew abreast of the camera, Johnson began waving the camera away. It was obvious he had seen the red light and knew what it meant. He stormed into the house and declared that we could pack up and leave. Again, Mrs. Johnson intervened, this time with help from Valenti and Brooks. Together they persuaded Johnson to let us finish, assuring him that the offending scene would be erased.

Another incident marred the day. Near the end of scheduled shooting, a crew member stepped backward and fell from a truck, hitting his head on a steel cattle guard. A deep gash bled profusely, and it was obvious he required medical attention. Mrs. Johnson had us put the casualty in one of the big white Lincolns, trademark of the LBJ Ranch, and her driver rushed him to the hospital in Johnson City, some fifteen miles away. Meantime, a ranch employee radioed the hospital that our man was coming.

The next day in Houston, Marich and Miller reviewed the raw footage and declared it to be excellent. We had plenty of usable material to fill an hour. Marich began editing. We had undertaken the project with a clear understanding the station had complete editorial control. We did agree, however, to preview the finished product for the vice-president. A time was set for Miller and me to meet with his group at Johnson's television station in Austin.

The night before, Marich announced he hadn't completed the edit but would stay late, so Ray and I could pick up the tape early next morning. When we arrived at our studios, Marich was still editing. Miller called Valenti, who was in Austin at the Johnson station, and reported the problem, but said Marich expected to finish in time for us to make the trip by car. As hours passed it became evident that driving to Austin was out of the question, so we contacted the private airfield at Sugar Land and arranged for a plane and pilot to stand by. When we called Valenti to report on progress, he explained that the vice-president was at the ranch and planned to stay there until Valenti was sure we were going to make it.

Finally, Marich handed us the tape. We raced to Sugar Land. Just before takeoff, Miller called Valenti to tell him we were on the way. Valenti said he would have one of the Johnson cars meet us at the transient terminal at Austin's airport. Fortunately, the flight was uneventful, and as we got into the car, the driver reported to Valenti that we were on the ground. He, in turn, notified the ranch, and the vice-president boarded his plane.

Meantime, Miller and I were driven to the downtown studios of the Johnson television station, where the tape was checked. While we waited for Johnson, we were told that his planned trip into Austin was not generally known. A testimonial dinner was scheduled that evening for Ralph Yarborough, the senior United States senator from Texas, who was no favorite of the vice-president. Johnson had declined an invitation to the dinner, so it would be embarrassing for him if it were known he was in the area.

Johnson arrived at the TV studio and the tape was played. The vice-president and those around him were quite pleased and warmly expressed their satisfaction. We were driven back to the airport, where our plane was waiting.

By then it was lunchtime, so our pilot taxied us across the field to the main terminal. The coffee shop offered a clear view of the gate area, and as we waited for our order, Yarborough's charter from Houston arrived. Among those deplaning were Adie Marks and Seymour "Slugger" Cohen, two close friends of mine and partners in the Houston advertising agency handling public relations for the senator. They left the main group and, entering the coffee shop, spotted us immediately. Naturally, they wanted to know what we were doing in Austin. While we fumbled for an answer, we could see Johnson's plane pull away from the transient terminal and head for the runway. I don't remember our explanation, and have never told Marks and Cohen this story.

We planned to offer the documentary for sponsorship, so I took a copy of the program to New York, where I met with members of Edward Petry & Company, a firm which has represented the KPRC stations to national advertisers and advertising agencies since the early days of broadcasting. A salesman from Petry and I viewed the tape with a number of prospects, and one expressed special interest but wouldn't make a commitment until a key executive returned to the city. I left my copy with the Petry salesman and flew home.

Then came November 22, and President Kennedy's assassination. Even as Lyndon Johnson was taking the oath of office in the cabin of Air Force One, parked on the runway at Dallas's Love Field, Jack Harris instructed Miller and Marich to begin reediting our documentary, which had not yet been telecast, for programming under these tragic, unforeseen circumstances. Then he called New York to offer the program to the network. NBC's staff was eager to have it. They realized the country as a whole knew little about the new president, and any substantive material about him would go a long way toward restoring confidence. We promised to let them know as soon as we had it ready.

Our Petry salesman in New York called to remind me that he also had a copy of the program. After checking with Jack Harris, I told him to walk it over to NBC. Harris called the network to tell them it was on the way. A short time later, but long enough for our representative to have made the short walk to Rockefeller Plaza, NBC called to ask Jack where the tape was. At that moment, pictures from the documentary came up on the NBC feed, and Harris suggested the NBC caller take a look at his own monitor. Somehow, in the confusion, our tape had bypassed normal network channels, but still reached someone who recognized its importance.

Over the next day or two, various excerpts from the Johnson documentary were played on NBC and other networks, and repeated over a number of local stations. In the opinion of serious observers, including many in the new president's administration, the program's insight into the thoughts of the man and his hopes for the country did much to restore the badly shaken morale of its people and ease the transition which had taken place so suddenly and tragically.

The program never played in its original form, but several years ago the original master tape, along with outtakes and the working tape itself, were delivered to the LBJ Library in Austin. The tapes are now stored in the archives, available to researchers and scholars. In preparing the material for the library, we discovered the scene in which Johnson returned to the ranch by plane after getting his hair cut. The segment had not been erased, and is now part of history.

Telethons

JACK HARRIS AND RON STONE

If Channel 2 didn't invent the telethon, a term coined from the words "television" and "marathon," it certainly was one of the first to try this modern form of fund-raising. The station was only sixteen months old, and still using the KLEE call letters, when it staged its first telethon on May 7, 1950. The five-hour program, telecast from the Shamrock Hotel, raised $28,000 for the American Cancer Society.

A little more than six months after Channel 2 became KPRC-TV, another telethon was scheduled. This one, from a theater in downtown Houston, was to benefit the March of Dimes. The results were disappointing, but we were beginning to learn that a parade of name entertainers was not enough. Local station personalities had to have dominant roles, and the effort must keep going almost to the point of exhaustion through the hours of darkness until well into the next afternoon. This January 1951 attempt closed down before daylight.

We put those lessons to use on April 19 and 20, 1952, when we originated from the Music Hall a telethon for the Cerebral Palsy Association. For the first time, we used our top local star, Dick Gottlieb, as master of ceremonies. As viewers watched him grow haggard from fatigue and listened to his increasingly hoarse pleadings, pledges and donations began to flow. The result was announced as $82,000, although later returns placed the final total nearer $100,000.

The next two telethons, June 13–14, 1953, and March 27–28,

83

1954, were sensationally successful for their day. Both were to benefit the Houston Lighthouse for the Blind. From the proceeds of the two broadcasts, the Lighthouse was able to buy land for a new workshop, build the facility, and completely equip it.

During the first of these two efforts, we invented a technique that has remained successful throughout telethons to follow. In the early predawn hours, pledges and contributions were slowing quite seriously. Paul Huhndorff, our chief engineer, suggested we open the studio door to the parking lot, put some lights and a camera in the doorway, and invite area residents to drive by, drop money in a barrel, and see themselves on television.

The idea worked so well we soon had cars lined up for miles in all directions, and the police had a difficult task keeping traffic moving. We called it the "Drive In, Drop In Barrel" or the "Fishbowl," and variations of it continue to be used.

Lighthouse for the Blind was a project of the Lions' Clubs, which put their best efforts into those telethons. The station's association with the Lions and Ray Elliot has continued through dozens of telethons since.

The 1955, 1956, and 1957 events, all held in mid-January, benefited the March of Dimes. In 1958 and 1959 we produced telethons for the Eyes of Texas Foundation, raising more than $160,000.

In 1964, over the Labor Day holiday, we presented a telethon for our old friends at Lighthouse for the Blind and raised $300,000; in 1965, our telethon benefited the Houston Muscular Dystrophy Association. We didn't know it at the time, but this latter relationship was going to be a longstanding one.

In 1970 MDA enlisted the aid of Jerry Lewis in organizing a nationwide network to televise an annual telethon over the Labor Day holiday. We were somewhat dubious about joining a multistation activity, since our most successful efforts had been undertaken independently. On the other hand, we had been at it long enough to know as much about telethons as anybody in the country, so we agreed to participate. And a whole new era began.

In most of our previous telethons, KPRC-TV originated the entire program, from beginning to end, including entertainment features as well as the frequent appeals and other special events. Now a good part of the entertainment portion would come from the network, along with appeals by Lewis and his big-name guests.

KPRC-TV and other participating stations would cut away from the network from time to time to make our own appeals and present local interest programming. It was during this first Jerry Lewis MDA telethon that a new element spontaneously entered the picture.

We were at the height of the so-called hippie period, when nothing seemed to "turn on" teenagers and other young people except an apparent obsession with drugs and demonstrations. At least, that's how it appeared to us of an older generation. Certainly nothing on television seemed to interest them.

But early on Labor Day, 1970, dozens of teenagers descended on our Post Oak studios. By midafternoon, they were there in the hundreds. They came in their dirty, tattered jeans, barefooted, with smudged faces and long hair. And they brought with them coffee cans filled with dollar bills and change. They sprawled on the floor in the lobby and in the corridors and counted their money. Then they emptied their coffee cans into the Fishbowl, and went back into the streets to collect more. From all over the city, entirely on their own and without any urging or organization, teens had gone from door to door collecting for "Jerry's Kids."

To this day, no one knows why it happened, but we count on the present generation of teenagers to be among the strongest supporters of the Muscular Dystrophy Association and the Labor Day telethon.

Dick Gottlieb, who had begun his long association with KPRC-TV's telethons in 1952, continued as our master of ceremonies through 1972, celebrating his twentieth anniversary on that year's program.

In 1973, after Gottlieb left the station, our principal news anchor, Steve Smith, served as master of ceremonies for the Labor Day telethon. Later that year, Smith joined a Pittsburgh television station. Ron Stone took over as our anchorman and as host for the annual MDA presentation. Ron claims he had no idea what he was in for:

> When Jack Harris hired me in December 1973, he casually "suggested" that I might be called on from time to time to "help out a little on the Labor Day thing." I did not know then but soon learned that Jack Harris can be a master of understatement.
>
> The "Labor Day thing" he was talking about was the Jerry Lewis Labor Day Telethon for Muscular Dystrophy, a project in

which he and KPRC-TV had been deeply involved from its very beginning in 1970. Since I had been in Houston television for several years before joining Channel 2, I knew about the Jerry Lewis telethon. In fact, everybody in Houston knew about the event. I also knew that Channel 2 had introduced this form of electronic fund-raising to Houston, had perfected it to the level of an art form, and had been spectacularly successful for a succession of worthy causes.

As September 1974 approached, I began to get the feeling my role was to be something more than "helping a little." Then came the realization that I was expected to play master of ceremonies for the entire affair. I was not unused to appearing in public. After all, I had been in radio and television for some time, and frequently spoke before groups around town. I confess, though, I have never been as scared in all my life.

As the evening and morning wore on, it seemed to me we were dealing with pure chaos. The big studio was jammed. I simply was not prepared for all the people and the pressure. More than once during those hours I wished I had stayed in Oklahoma to raise turkeys. Then, little by little, it all began to make sense.

Fourteen pledge centers had been set up throughout the area served by the station. We called them the "Love Network," and the system worked well. Somehow, Jack Harris and Tom Reiff got me through it, and the 1974 telethon set a new record. We raised almost three-quarters of a million dollars — $749,973, to be exact.

During the following year the Muscular Dystrophy Association program began to bring tangible results to Houston. MDA opened the Jerry Lewis Neuromuscular Research Center in Texas Medical Center, and the Gulf Chapter of MDA began a camp program, calling it the Bill Enis Muscular Dystrophy Summer Camp. Bill, before his death from a heart attack in late 1973, had been the popular and well-loved sportscaster on KPRC-TV. He participated in several of the telethons, including the one in 1973.

We had a great telethon in 1975. The money poured in, and we passed the previous year's $750,000 mark early Labor Day afternoon. Pledges kept growing, and as we neared the end, Kirt Harriss, our promotion and research director and "man about everything," walked up to me with a bucket of yellow paint in one hand and a paintbrush in the other. Just then we took a cut-in, breaking the network feed for a local update, and Jack Harris announced we had broken a million dollars. I took the yellow paint and painted a huge "1" on the tote board, then Kirt and I stood back with tears in our eyes. It was the proudest moment of my broadcast career.

In 1976 we realized the telethon had outgrown our studios, so we moved to the Astro Arena. And disaster struck! A major wind and rain storm blew in, and sometime in the middle of the night the phones stopped ringing. I begged and pleaded and used every trick I could think of, but nothing worked. Then we discovered the phones were out of service, and for the next six hours we played telethon without phones. In first light of dawn Jack Harris came to me and calmly, but firmly, told me we were going to turn the disaster to our advantage. I was to explain the phone problem, then appeal to the community for extra help once the phones were back in order. It worked. Our total by that evening was $1,239,038!

In 1977 MDA funded a million dollars to establish the Jack Harris Research Unit of the Jerry Lewis Neuromuscular Disease Research Center, a well-earned recognition for the man who, more than any other, made Labor Day telethons in Houston a benchmark for the rest of the country. That year we moved the telethon to the Summit. Our pledges totaled $1,489,603.

In the eighteen years KPRC-TV has participated in the Jerry Lewis Labor Day Telethon, Houston area viewers have contributed over $25 million for muscular dystrophy research and to assist victims of neuromuscular diseases. Year by year, here is the tally:

1970	$ 294,424	1980	$2,010,931
1971	$ 340,404	1981	$2,030,283
1972	$ 385,143	1982	$1,906,386
1973	$ 533,187	1983	$2,005,067
1974	$ 749,973	1984	$1,915,521
1975	$1,283,000	1985	$1,730,602
1976	$1,239,038	1986	$1,632,117
1977	$1,489,603	1987	$1,749,788
1978	$1,513,137	1988	$1,769,171
1979	$1,658,399		

KPRC has produced and participated in other telethons during those years. There were the early United Negro College Fund efforts that showed the way for a national UNCF telethon. In 1979, and again in 1980, at the specific urgent request of Bob Hope, we did two telethons for the benefit of Hughen School for the Handicapped at Port Arthur, and fed the programs to a regional network. Hope himself was master of ceremonies from our studios. And in 1980 and 1981, we shared in a joint effort with the other Houston stations to secure blood donations.

The Labor Day telethons for muscular dystrophy have touched us most deeply, and we have dedicated our greatest efforts to Jerry's Kids. They've known the tragedy and heartbreak of these diseases from experience. These courageous children and men and women have volunteered to work with us through the long nights and days of the holiday weekends, as much to help others as themselves. Ron Stone spoke for all KPRC-TV's staff when he recently wrote:

> Greg Shry's photograph hangs on our coffee shop wall filled with mementos from the Muscular Dystrophy Association. Each time I pass that wall I think of that young man.
>
> He was our poster kid, and a wonderful ambassador for MDA and Channel 2. One year Greg and I rode in an antique fire truck in a downtown parade. They loaded him and his wheelchair on the truck, and I climbed into the seat beside the driver. As we wound our way through the streets, Greg and I waved to an enthusiastic crowd. At one point, the poster kid said, "Boy, they all know me and are waving. I bet they wonder who that old man in the front seat is." Greg died the next year. I told that story at his funeral and the crowd in the church in Alvin laughed aloud. It was the first time I ever heard laughter at a funeral. Greg's mother, Mary Ann, continues to be a volunteer at every one of our telethons.
>
> Michelle Franke was a bright young poster child when I first saw her at a telethon. I had been warned not to get too closely attached to the children because they had little chance of growing past their teen years. But MD research, made possible by our telethon, has changed that. Today Michelle is a college senior, and when I see her now she tells me about her boyfriends, her grades, her hopes for the future.
>
> When I first met them, Frankie and "Slugger" were twisted, skeletal young men, slumped in their wheelchairs. Their mother, Delores Lindsay, staged a Labor Day auction in the little town of Old Ocean, and at each telethon appeared near the end of the program with a little green suitcase filled with cash. To see Delores through my haze of fatigue, in the final hours of the program, was enough to give me an instant shot of adrenalin.
>
> Both her sons died; first Slugger, then, a year later, Frankie. Delores asked me to speak at their funerals. It was the most difficult thing I have ever had to do. Here is a part of what I said at Frankie's funeral:
>
> "I have always admired courage. With the Lindsays, I have

seen it firsthand. I cannot stand here and recite a list of Frankie's accomplishments in a world that judges people by what they can do. I can say to those who knew him better than I, that what he did was far greater than anyone can imagine. And you know that is true.

"I don't know whether he ever wanted to run the 440. I don't know whether he ever wanted to ride a bull. I don't know whether he ever wanted to be an astronaut. I don't know whether he ever wanted to just settle down to be a working man.

"I know he never had a chance to do any of those things. And I know that made him sad. I know that for most of his too-short life he knew pain, and dejection, and finally, defeat. But I know he also understood and received something most of us get precious little of — love. Love from his parents, his relatives, from people he never knew.

"It was received, I think, because he had a genuine capacity to love. I don't think he ever asked why his mother and father put up with so much to make him comfortable. I don't think he ever asked why people in this community helped make the Lindsay boys famous by their giving on Labor Day. I think he just knew we cared. All of us. And he showed he cared with that smile. Not so much in his lips, but in his eyes. I never saw defeat in them. I saw tired. I saw disgusted. Sometimes, I saw boredom. But never defeat!

"He knew, as we all did, what would happen. And it happened, finally.

"Let me look past the casket to the family. What brave people you are, and have been. Someone once said, 'God never gives you more than you can stand,' and I said, 'Delores Lindsay proved that.' I don't know how you coped. But you did. Now, no one can say more than: we are sorry the fight is over. But how well you helped the boys fight!''

Five Documentary Films

LOIS FARFEL STARK

In the last half of the 1970s, I was privileged to write and produce five major KPRC-TV documentary films on topics inextricably bound with the future of Houston.

Three of the five were concerned with medicine. For most of the world, the Texas Medical Center is every bit as familiar as the Johnson Space Center, and work being done there rates headlines in medical journals on every continent. The first of the series, "Cures to Come: Medical Research," focused on current medical research which would affect the next decade. We explored space spin-offs, the first phase of cancer immunology tests, memory implant experimentation, the politics of medical funding, and national priorities in the health field. We were encouraged and assisted by the M.D. Anderson complex and Baylor College of Medicine. We also had access to world-renowned authorities including Dr. Michael Debakey.

The second documentary in this series, "Out of Mind; Out of Sight," was a critical examination of publicly supported facilities which care for the mentally ill. It is still a viable topic. The program discussed institutional overloads, legal complications, and shortcomings in medical knowledge and practice in the field of mental illness. "Out of Mind; Out of Sight" won an award from the Texas Association of Broadcasters.

The third medical documentary was "Dedicated to Life; The Texas Medical Center." It was our intention to dramatize what the medical center means to Houston. We demonstrated its economic impact as Houston's largest employer. We related its unique history, the story of a group of Houston civic leaders who created a federation of institutions with two common bonds: their professional concern with the health of mankind, and their joint occupancy of what was once a wilderness tract on the outskirts of town.

We reported the Texas Medical Center's international reputation, how it attracted patients and researchers from around the world. We described the unsurpassed research facilities, where dedicated men and women work to further extend our knowledge of medicine. This film is still shown regularly by Texas Medical Center and the University of Houston.

The other two programs turned to the city at large. "We Are What We Build" related the city's architecture to its character, its values, and its place in time. The way the modern city is laid out reveals much of its economic history. The wide downtown streets, for instance, were planned to be broad enough to permit a horse-drawn lumber wagon to make a U-turn. After lumber, cotton was king, then came the oil boom, bringing a procession of refineries and chemical plants along the ship channel and sparkling midtown skyscraper headquarters. The city's growth was dictated by its flatland location, by the development of practical air conditioning, by the demands of the automobile, and by its inhabitants' rugged individualism.

We explained the differing points of view held by a building's architect, the developer of the complex, the corporate entity that will occupy it, the construction worker who helps build it, and the man on the street who watches it grow. We listened to the debate among champions of urban renewal, historic preservation, zoning and planning. We followed the benchmarks of growth along Westheimer, from the recycled Montrose mansions of the thirties, through the fashion malls of the sixties, to the highway sign-dominated, automobile-oriented lifestyle of the eighties.

After it was shown on KPRC-TV, this documentary was requested for private screenings by architectural, civic, and urban planning groups throughout the United States, quoted in architectural periodicals, and presented at the Museum of Fine Arts in Houston and the American Center in Paris.

Finally, we produced "Houston: The International City." Houston had barely become accustomed to its place among the great cities of the United States before it became an international city. The oil industry played a major role in this process, typified by the flags of dozens of nations flying from tankers in the Houston Ship Channel and the millions of dollars of foreign investment in Houston's petroleum-related businesses. We pointed out Houston landmarks now owned by foreign investors, and the thousands of visitors the city welcomes each year, ranging from students to medical patients to heads of state. We remarked on the growing number of foreign consulates and financial institutions; the United Nations mix at every economic level; the influx of Vietnamese; and the fact that ninety-eight languages are spoken in Houston's public schools.

"Houston: The International City" won a CINE Golden Eagle award and was selected to represent the United States in several foreign film events. The Library of Congress requested a copy for its catalog; the University of Houston, the Houston Chamber of Commerce, and several foreign countries also asked for copies. American Women in Radio and Television honored the film with their highest Matrix award.

The photographer, director, and editor for all these programs was Fred Schultze of the KPRC-TV staff. Narrator for "Cures to Come: Medical Research" was John Flynn. The other four programs were narrated by Ron Stone.

The Selling Game

JACK McGREW

Unlike their counterparts in many nations, most radio and television stations in the United States derive all of their operating revenues from commercial advertising. So-called "public" broadcasting operations did not arrive on the scene until fairly late, and even they now look to rather thinly disguised commercial messages for much of their operating budget.

Television had the distinct advantage of inheriting from radio an already well-developed business structure that made the American system of commercial broadcasting work. At the local level, stations had their own sales organizations that called upon local advertisers and/or their advertising agencies. At regional and national levels, stations appointed exclusive sales representatives with offices in major buying centers across the country, staffed to call upon regional and national advertisers and/or their advertising agencies. These reps were compensated by commissions on advertising they sold.

Stations, wherever possible, made affiliations with one or more of the nationwide or regional broadcasting networks that supplied the most popular entertainment programming and, like the stations, supported their organization and their programming efforts with advertising revenues. From this income, networks maintained elaborate facilities and compensated affiliated stations for time occupied by network programming. Network sales departments often solicited the same advertisers and/or advertising agen-

93

cies as the various local station sales reps. Now and then a station would discover it was, in a sense, competing with itself.

Network compensation to stations was calculated upon a far different and less favorable basis than was developed by the station for its own local and national sales. A network affiliate in a major market like Houston could, and often did, discover that ninety-five percent or more of its operating income came from local, regional, and national direct sales, with five percent or less coming from the network payments. At the same time, seventy or eighty percent or more of the station's available air time might be occupied by network programming.

Again, the value of network affiliation far outweighed the seeming imbalance. The primary advantages were having the audience developed for the station by network programming and the tremendous saving to the station in not having to purchase or produce huge blocks of expensive entertainment programming.

It was this structure that television inherited and adapted, a process made much easier because so many early TV stations were put into service by experienced radio station operators and managers with longstanding associations with sales representatives and networks. They simply carried these customs and associations into the new medium. Edward Petry and Company, KPRC Radio's longtime sales representative, was soon appointed to represent the television station as well. In time, after other stations were licensed to the market, KPRC-TV became Houston's exclusive affiliate of the NBC television network.

By the time television came along, Houston was already one of the country's most vigorous and prosperous markets, served by an array of highly competitive network-affiliated and independent radio stations and by three major metropolitan daily newspapers. Virtually every home had at least one radio receiver. This often imposing piece of furniture, able to receive both AM and FM broadcasts, occupied a place of honor in the living or family room. Television receivers were so rare in the first years as to become immediate neighborhood curiosities.

Proud owners of TV sets found friends and neighbors dropping in, often without invitation, to peer for hours into a tiny round screen, often smeared with "snow," peopled by correspondingly tiny, dimly seen actors, singers, and dancers. Commercials were equally primitive. Often a photographic slide or series of slides would accompany what was, in fact, a radio commercial announcement. Early television cartoon characters that moved with clumsy, spastic animation competed with live action spots with stilted story lines.

Houston was uncharacteristically slow to respond to the new medium. Potential viewers held back, perhaps, by misgivings about its staying power and long-term prospects, by unfamiliarity with Channel 2's original licensee as a broadcaster, and, certainly, by the very high cost of early television receivers. Even so, those early owners of TV sets weren't necessarily prosperous. As often as not, they were middle- and lower-income families who saw the new medium as an alternative to the movie theater and figured they could pay for the newfangled device with money saved by staying home nights and watching television.

Houston advertisers were also skittish. They, too, were unfamiliar and perhaps uncomfortable with the station's operator in this new role, and were certainly uneasy about television with the new technical demands and confusing jargon. Most advertisers were painfully conscious that TV operators were also just beginning to learn the new business. The advertisers were very aware of the limited size of the television audience and had no idea of the makeup of that small audience in terms of likely buyers for their goods and services.

The advertising rates were certainly modest enough. During the first year of operation, Channel 2's highest price for a one-minute announcement was $50. The new management immediately doubled the price when the station became KPRC-TV, and created consternation among more than a few of the advertisers. The new rate of $100 per minute was generally considered as fair, however, when compared to the charges for radio commercial time.

A few people at both the agency and client level did recognize television as a new marketing tool of virtually unlimited promise. Governor and Mrs. Hobby and the senior executives of the KPRC organization also saw the wide-open opportunity.

Tentatively at first, Houston's advertisers began to experiment with television. One classic tale involved the housewares section of a major national retail chain. The local manager was instructed to lay in a larger supply of ordinary white house paint so a television marketing test could be conducted. A "reasonable" announcement schedule was ordered. There was to be no other advertising of the paint or the price, just television, and the price quoted for the paint in the television ads was not extraordinary. The ads showed up on the air the night before the sale was to begin. By noon of that first day, the supply of paint was exhausted, and an embarrassed, flustered manager complained to the advertising department that he was going to need a lot more notice and a much larger inventory the next time the store planned to promote a product on television.

A modest-sized Houston advertising agency, sensing television's potential, had considerable success soliciting business from Houston companies. Armed with the orders to buy television time, the agency began firming up sizable blocks of desirable commercial time, adjacent to or within the more popular programs. Eventually the larger, more conservative advertising agencies became frustrated by their inability to deliver comparable time segments to their clients. In some cases, they began to lose clients to the upstart agency that had the available time under contract, and they began to accuse the station of playing favorites among the ad community. Reasonably enough, station managers pointed out that the same initial opportunity had existed for all. It appeared to be a clear-cut case of initiative being properly rewarded.

The situation that caused the "ad war" was simply that KPRC-TV was the only television station in the area, a circumstance that lasted for several years. It was a situation with drawbacks for the station, as well. All four early networks, NBC, CBS, ABC, and Dumont, claimed Channel 2 as an affiliate, making it possible for the station to pick and choose from all of the programming available, but it also made for some strange time periods for some very popular shows. There was a lot of audience resentment about the scheduling, both in the show selection and the choices of time period. Every early set owner considered he was also pioneering in the business and assumed the right to help dictate the program schedule. Advertisers, who were paying the bills, often felt the same way.

Then there was the problem of live programming, including the commercials. Some of the biggest disasters of early telecasting occurred during the commercials or involved the client's products. One very popular local program was Jane Christopher's "TV Kitchen," five days a week, fifty-two weeks a year, and even when Jane went on vacation every summer.

Her summer replacements were two of the station's young staff announcers, Bob Dundas and Lee Gordon. When they took over, the cookbooks and the timers and the dedication to the culinary arts went out the door right behind the vacation-bound Jane. Bob and Lee were two bulls in a china shop but, ironically enough, their two-week summer show was a big crowd pleaser.

A major manufacturer of kitchen ranges supplied the latest model for Jane's use on the set. The manufacturer's chief executive officer happened to be in town and watching television in his hotel room the day Bob and Lee decided to toss some bacon on the stove at the beginning of the show. They tossed three pounds of bacon on the stove, then turned their backs and started stirring and mixing another dish. Within moments the set was beginning to fill up with smoke. The bacon was sizzling. Then it was charring — all three pounds of it.

The smoke got thicker. The cameramen backed up, then stepped away. Bob and Lee played the moment for all it was worth — until the president of the appliance company got on the telephone from his hotel room and began demanding that the show be stopped and his company's gas range be disconnected and returned, forthwith.

Eventually, the crisis passed. The appliance maker was mollified, and the ratings of "TV Kitchen" continued to increase. That's when Bob and Lee dumped an entire can of popcorn into a hot skillet, then had to abandon the set as popcorn began flying in all directions, an inevitable process that went on for the rest of the scheduled half-hour.

KPRC-TV's national sales representative, Edward Petry and Company, was confronted with some unique challenges and came up with some very unorthodox solutions to Houston TV's early problems. The demand for commercial time on Houston's only television station made for some stiff competition on the national level, and once a salesman had an advertising schedule accepted by the station, he made every effort to protect it.

The generally accepted industry rule was that a spot must be reconfirmed at least two weeks before the order expired or it was fair game for anybody who had a buyer standing by. A New York Petry salesman had a schedule of auto-maker spots running on KPRC-TV. The schedule was nearing the two-week danger period and the salesman was unable to contact the agency buyer, who was also the agency media director, and who, according to his secretary, was terribly busy with other matters.

No amount of telephoning seemed to help and dropping by the man's office didn't work, so the resourceful salesman resorted to his secret weapon. Over the years, he had become friendly with a counterman in the ground-floor quick-lunch restaurant in his office building. Besides the counter traffic and carry-out business, the restaurant did a thriving trade sending out coffee, donuts, and other snacks on a push cart that made stops all over the neighborhood. The salesman persuaded the counterman to loan him a push cart and the white jacket and cap that went with it. He even bought enough merchandise to make a decent showing.

Properly disguised, the salesman pushed the cart up Madison Avenue to Fifty-third Street, then west half a block to the brownstone building that had been remodeled to serve as the ad agency's headquarters. Since he was well-known to the ground floor receptionist, he averted his head as he pushed his cart through the lobby.

The buyer's office was on the third floor in the front of the building and the elevator was at the other end of the corridor. The salesman played his act to the hilt, actually making a few sales as he moved down the hallway to the elevator, then pushed the button for the third floor. There he started back down the corridor, again making sales as he went. Finally, he reached the buyer's door. The man looked up, noted the familiar push cart and uniform, then casually ordered black coffee and a Danish.

The salesman prepared the order, walked over to the desk, and put the pastry and coffee in front of the buyer. Then he took off the cap and said, "Tom, I need to talk to you about that Packard schedule in Houston."

The startled buyer looked up, finally recognizing the man from the Petry company, and started laughing. The salesman got the spot schedule renewed.

Some early advertisers secured what would eventually become franchise positions in Houston television. Foley's is a perfect example. In the early fifties its single, five-story, downtown location was the city's leading department store, and the company had been a longtime, successful user of radio advertising. Foley's picked up full sponsorship of the first quarter-hour of the 10:00 P.M. TV newscast, three nights a week.

Even though full program sponsorship ended in the seventies,

Foley's still retains partial sponsorship of Channel 2's 10:00 P.M. news. It is the oldest continuing relationship with any television program in Houston. In fact, neither station records nor those of Foley's reflect the actual start date, so no one knows how long Foley's has sponsored the evening news on KPRC-TV.

There are still viewers around who fondly remember some of those early live Foley's commercials. There was the time announcer Lee Gordon was extolling the virtues of men's walking shorts and serving as his own on-camera model. Lee got a quick glimpse of himself, knobby knees and all, on a studio monitor, and began to giggle. He choked and gurgled a good fifteen seconds longer than the spot was supposed to run, but never did get to the essential information, the price.

Lee's one great failing was also his greatest strength. He knew how to laugh at himself. He just couldn't control the time and place it would start to happen — in spite of frequent "discussions" with Jack Harris. His on-the-air gaffes became another early tradition.

On one occasion he was demonstrating a new model refrigerator with a large freezer compartment that rolled out from the bottom third of the appliance for easy access. Lee was wearing the customary "lavalier" microphone of the time, draped around the neck of his dress shirt by a strong nylon cord, with the microphone cable concealed beneath his suit jacket. Lee stooped to one knee and rolled the freezer compartment out for inspection, made his sales point, then gently pushed the roll-out drawer closed — and got his microphone cord tangled in the mechanism.

For a good ten seconds Lee attempted to struggle to his feet, only managing to completely lose his composure. The camera stayed fixed on his predicament. Finally, in an unrehearsed imitation of Al Jolson, Lee managed to deliver the punch line — crouched on one knee with face pressed against the refrigerator door.

It was a memorable moment. The refrigerator sold well and Lee, forgiven by his audience, continued to make live television more interesting.

An aspect of television station operation that receives almost no notice outside the industry, and frequently not enough notice inside the business, is traffic — the placement of commercial spots within the day's programming. It sounds like a simple, mechanical task, but traffic is a critical area. Sponsors try to buy specific times and then expect to have their promotional spots or sales messages telecast at the specific times, within or adjacent to programming that interests an audience also attracted to the product or service offered in the commercials. With only so many commercial minutes available in a day and a variety of competing products to advertise, the opportunity for misfortune and conflict is substantial.

From radio experience, the management of KPRC-TV knew from the beginning that traffic control is a key element to success. Carelessness, ignorance, indifference, or (in rare instances) undue pressure from salespeople anxious to please a favored client will inevitably result in costly mistakes. The wrong message is telecast or the right message is placed in the wrong time slot. An announcement is placed too close to that of a competitor (no longer the taboo it once was), or an announcement is missed altogether. These errors cost money, and they can cost reputation. Sure, such mistakes can be "made up," if the advertiser is willing, but nobody pays for the time that was used when the error was made. And if such incidents occur very often, the advertiser may well take his business elsewhere.

Stations have lost hundreds of thousands of dollars due to poor traffic management. Even worse, a reputation for sloppy handling spreads quickly along Madison Avenue and can make life very tough for sales representatives.

Good traffic management has always been a priority with the KPRC stations and, from the beginning of television in Houston, KPRC-TV has had the services of dedicated, knowledgeable, industrious, and meticulously honest traffic managers and assistants. These people have tended to stick with the job. In forty years of operation, there have been only five traffic managers, an unsurpassed record of continuity.

KPRC-TV actually created and perfected several now standard sales concepts. In cooperation with the Petry organization, also an innovator, we helped introduce the grid rate card, sometimes referred to as the "demand" card. In the beginning, television had adopted what was then the radio rate card structure. Commercials in a general block of time were priced the same, regardless of the popularity of individual programs within those time blocks. Discounts were allowed for frequency of use or the number of units ordered.

As television audiences increased and became more selective, advertisers and their agencies became more sophisticated and re-search-oriented. Positions adjacent to the most popular programs, especially those with the kinds of audience most nearly matching needs of large mass-marketing advertisers, were filled almost im-mediately. Other positions in the same general time block often went unsold. The process was called "cherry-picking."

The grid card was designed to correct this imbalance by pric-ing each announcement position on its individual merits as re-ported by the rating services and as perceived by the advertising community. Rates were adjusted from time to time to reflect changing program tastes, audience fluctuations, viewer composi-tion, market alterations, and competitive conditions.

The concept seems simple today, but when first introduced, the grid system was difficult to sell to buyers long accustomed to rigid, seldom-changed rate structures. The station sales manager tried explaining the concept to his wife, who immediately grasped the idea. "It's just like paying more for ten pounds of potatoes than for five," she said.

In order to gain acceptance for the rate plan, Channel 2 sales and the Petry reps conducted clinics in a number of Southwestern markets for agency/advertiser staffs and for other station manage-ment and sales people. Advantages for both station and client be-came increasingly apparent. On the one hand, the station was fi-nally able to receive true worth for its highest- rated adjacencies; on the other, the advertiser and his agency were assured of receiving actual value for their dollars in terms of measurable numbers of po-tential customers. Thus was born "cost per thousand," the cost for reaching 1,000 viewing homes.

Today's television prices are developed from this "CPM" con-cept. For two 30-second announcement positions in and adjacent to the 1985 Super Bowl, Channel 2 required $35,000. For adjacencies to the weekly "Bill Cosby Show," Channel 2's thirty-second rate, as of January 1988, was $11,000 per announcement. Yet another prime-time network spot next to a less popular show on another night might sell for as little as $2,000. Comparison to the $100-per-spot rates of 1950 shows how far television sales have come.

Under the grid card, a single position might be offered at sev-eral different levels: a premium "fixed" rate, at which an advertiser would be guaranteed the announcement would run as ordered; a "pre-emptible" rate, at which the advertiser might be preempted on two weeks' notice in favor of an advertiser willing to pay the fixed rate; and a still lower "immediately pre-emptible" rate, at which an advertiser might be bumped without any notice by another advertiser willing to pay either of the two higher charges. The networks, and many stations, went a step further. In order to justify rates which might seem out of line for new and untested programming, they began guaranteeing audiences, both as to size and composition, and offering "make-goods" to compensate when actual audience figures fell short of projections.

The number of commercial positions that can be scheduled within a certain time frame, or even throughout an entire broadcast day, may seem infinite to the outsider, but is in fact limited. To the surprise of no one, some of these variations led to abuses and, in extreme cases, to complete disruption of otherwise carefully designed marketing plans. Some of the other rate card designs led to situations in which the station might suddenly find itself sold out at rates lower than those its competitors were then able to secure.

With a mature understanding of the nature of the business, and convinced rate-making was the only practical tool for a station to control its inventory, KPRC-TV adopted a policy giving advertisers the assurance that their schedules would be run as ordered, fulfilling part of an overall marketing plan. By maintaining a close watch on unsold positions still in the future, and by adjusting rates accordingly, the station could also secure a fair price for services and protect the flexibility to manage "inventory." A good part of the commercial success of the station, and of the respect in which KPRC-TV is held by the advertising community, is due to consistent implementation of that policy.

Early on, KPRC-TV also pledged to provide its employees with an opportunity to step into more challenging (and more financially rewarding) roles. Several key management people have moved into or through sales from other departments of the station. "Katy" Estes moved into traffic management from the promotion department of Channel 2 in the mid-1950s. She became one of the first female executives in the business when she was later promoted to national sales manager. Such advancement not only improves morale within the organization, but also strengthens the station by broadening the hands-on experience of its staff.

"Houston, The *Eagle* Has Landed!"

PAUL HUHNDORFF

Establishment of the Manned Spacecraft Center (MSC) at Clear Lake, between Houston and Galveston, brought Houston and KPRC-TV into the United States space program. The early experimental unmanned and manned suborbital and orbital flights had been launched and controlled from Cape Canaveral, on Florida's east coast, south of Daytona Beach. But when the National Aeronautics and Space Administration (NASA) opened its giant development, training, and control facility on what used to be grazing land between Webster and Seabrook, the attention of a space-conscious world shifted to Texas.

The second manned Gemini flight, so named because the vehicle carried two astronauts into an orbital trip around earth, was launched June 3, 1965, from Cape Canaveral. Immediately after launch, control of the flight shifted to the Clear Lake complex. In preparation for this step forward in the space program, NBC contracted with KPRC-TV to build, equip, and staff a permanent studio on top of the Nassau Bay Hotel, just across the highway from the space center complex. NBC News anchors Chet Huntley and David Brinkley reported both the space flight and the afternoon news from the "Bubble," with a view of the Manned Spacecraft Center over their shoulders.

Gemini 4 was a rousing success and created a permanent assignment for Channel 2. From that mission through the *Challenger* tragedy in January 1986, KPRC-TV has provided the equipment and staff making it possible for television viewers across the country

103

and around the world to witness the exploration of space. Our crews covered the remainder of the Gemini program, the Apollo effort which put men on the moon, the Skylab series, the Apollo-Soyuz linking, and every shuttle mission.

In order to reduce the number of people and amount of equipment required for network coverage, and to lighten demands on NASA personnel, NBC, ABC, and CBS agreed among themselves to rotate "pool" coverage. Each network, in turn, assumed responsibility to the others for all except its own unilateral pickups.

All three networks contracted with KPRC-TV to handle the pool assignment as each took its turn. We also regularly handled NBC's own unique origination, and sometimes did special assignments for CBS and ABC. As other countries became directly involved, we began doing origination for television networks around the world, thus becoming even more a part of our country's space effort. The job has never become routine.

The setup for a normal mission might include one camera and a videotape machine in the pool area, one camera and audio equipment in Building 30 (the control center), and a camera and audio equipment at the home of each astronaut. Since we had to maintain our local operations at our studios and elsewhere, we often found it necessary to rent additional equipment and employ extra specialists. To provide enough remote units, for example, we hired trucks and added air conditioning to keep our electronics, and our people, cool.

There were twelve missions in the Gemini program; then came six unmanned orbital tests of the Apollo equipment. That vehicle was designed to carry three astronauts to the moon and back, and to act as mother ship for a lunar lander, which would actually ferry two astronauts to the surface of the moon, then return to the command module. NASA experienced its first directly space-related fatalities during this testing interval. In January 1967, a flash fire in a training capsule killed astronauts Gus Grissom, Ed White, and Roger Chaffee.

On October 11, 1968, "Wally" Schirra, Don Eisele, and Walter Cunningham climbed aboard *Apollo 7,* known to the astronauts as "Mission C," for a successful manned earth orbital test of machines and procedures. Just over two months later, December 12, 1968, *Apollo 8,* with astronauts Frank Borman, James Lovell, and William Anders aboard, roared upwards on a *Saturn V* rocket for man's first venture beyond his own planet. During this flight, on Christmas Eve, Borman, circling the moon in the command module, read: "In the beginning God created the heaven and the earth . . ." No one who heard it will ever forget.

Apollo 9, beginning March 3, 1969, provided a test, in earth orbit, of the undocking and docking procedure designed to separate the lunar lander from its command module and enable it to maneuver in space, then return. Astronauts James McDivott, David Scott, and Russell Schweickart carried it off successfully.

Apollo 10 was the final rehearsal. On May 18, 1969, Thomas Stafford, John Young, and Eugene Cernan lifted off in a spacecraft nicknamed *Charlie Brown.* During the flight, Stafford and Cernan flew the lunar lander *Snoopy* to within nine miles of the moon's surface, then rendezvoused with the command module for their return to earth. They proved it could be done.

The July 16 launch date for *Apollo 11* had been set weeks earlier, and the crew, Neil Armstrong, Michael Collins, and Edwin "Buzz" Aldrin, had been named months before. The command module, abbreviated to CSM, was christened *Columbia,* and the lunar lander, the LM, was called *Eagle.* On June 12 the critical decision was made to launch as scheduled.

Our own countdown began June 27. We were handling the pool for CBS, exclusive feeds for NBC, and servicing the Mexican network Telesistema, the Japanese NHK network, the BBC for Great Britain, Italy's RAI system, and the EBU system for all the rest of Europe. On June 27 we began loading sets to be moved to the Nassau Bay Hotel, and on June 30, we transferred the first batch of equipment. The same day, CBS shipped in 1,500 feet of cable for installation in NASA's Building 37, where the astronauts were to be quarantined following their return from the moon. From June 30 through July 4, we were also assembling single-camera remote units in the three trucks assigned to the astronauts' homes.

From July 7 through July 12, we were busy installing equipment for both the pool and NBC. We made arrangements to rent cameras and other components from KLRU, The University of Texas station in Austin, and WDSU in New Orleans. During the same week we set up two VTR trucks, one for the network pool and the other for the EBU system. On July 11 we dispatched a truck to Austin to pick up monitors and a microwave for the crash unit, a prototype of the ENG units which would become a fixture of news operations years later. We also furnished lights for Building 1 and Building 30, for Room 623 at the Nassau Bay Hotel, and for each of the astronaut home locations.

On July 12 and 13 we put the rented cameras in place and sent three cameras from our studios to Clear Lake, and on July 14 set up cameras at each astronaut residence. We went through a full facilities checkout on July 15 and pronounced ourselves ready for next day's liftoff.

Millions of words have been spoken or written about the flight of *Apollo 11*, but to those of us who watched at NASA center, it will always hold a special meaning. I think we all felt we were a part of history when, at 3:18 Sunday afternoon, July 20, 1969, Neil Armstrong said, "Houston, Tranquility Base here. The *Eagle* has landed."

That was the message everyone was waiting for, and Channel 2 relayed it to the world! Almost six and a half hours later, while viewers around the globe watched pictures we were sending from Houston control, Armstrong stepped from the foot of the LM's ladder to the moon's dusty surface and announced, "That's one small step for man, one giant leap for mankind!" The time in Houston was 9:56 P.M.

We had been at full strength at the Manned Spacecraft Center since early morning, and would remain at full strength until late the following day. That meant there would be little relief for our crews for about thirty-six hours. We had arranged for campers so they could catch a few minutes of rest whenever an opportunity occurred.

At 12:55 P.M. on Monday, July 21, *Eagle* lifted off from the surface of the moon. Less than four hours later, at 4:30 P.M., the two spacecraft were linked, still in orbit, and Armstrong and Aldrin were preparing to reenter the command module. It was near midnight Monday, while *Columbia* was on the backside of the moon and out of radio contact with Houston control, that the engine burned briefly to send the spacecraft out of lunar orbit and back toward earth. Almost sixty hours later, at 11:45 A.M., Thursday, July 24, *Columbia* splashed down in the Pacific, near the carrier *Hornet*. Our astronauts were taken aboard almost immediately and placed in an isolation capsule. Outside the capsule to greet them was President Richard Nixon. The entire mission had followed a flight plan prepared months in advance and timed almost to the second.

The rocks Armstrong and Aldrin collected while they were on the moon were flown directly to Houston. We had a camera in Building 37's Rock Quarantine Room when they arrived. But what we and the rest of the world were really waiting for was the astronauts themselves. They came at 1:00 A.M., Sunday, July 27, to Ellington Field. We were there. My memo, written weeks before, read:

> They [the astronauts] will arrive at Ellington at 1 A.M. on the 27th, be transported to Building 37 and arrive there about 3 A.M. Now!! We are to cover the arrival with two cameras (cam truck with pool switcher). Also, we are to have two cameras installed in Room 190 in Building 37. Also one of the cameras that is to go in the Room (190) will be used on the outside near the entrance where the truck docks and unloads the quarantine capsule. After the arrival, the camera moves inside. Equipment will have to be assembled in a truck. If there are any questions, ask them. There is no need to tell you this is a big job, but I know that you can do it and you can feel that you played an integral part in putting a man on the moon!

Like the mission, our coverage went according to plan. The *Apollo 11* flight required eleven microwave systems in and out of our studios, so all nations of the world could be fed signals. We had a total of sixty-four people working during the flight; forty-five of these were from our staff. Others were hired from stations in Austin and elsewhere. Charges to the networks and others we served during the mission totaled $230,000.

The Apollo program continued. The next flight, *Apollo 12*, manned by Pete Conrad, Alan Bean, and Richard Gordon, went wonderfully well. That could not be said for *Apollo 13*, which was launched April 11, 1970, carrying James Lovell, John Swigert, and Fred Haise. The flight lifted off routinely, and most of our staff had been released to wait out the long, tedious voyage to the moon.

Channel 2 had also been asked by NBC to provide the crew for the pickup in the Southwest Pacific — the first time a local station had ever been assigned that coverage. Because of the number of men assigned to the pickup crew, we had recruited several outside camera operators and engineers to fill out the roster of crew people at the MSC. Bill Parrott, one of our own cameramen, had recommended a friend of his from Austin, John Shives, to fill in as a location engineer. These two men, along with Channel 2 engineer

Tom Karonica, had taken advantage of the downtime to get together for an "old army buddy" reunion at Bill's apartment.

While they swapped stories and reminiscences, the television set was tuned to ABC, and a remark by that network's science reporter caught Parrott's attention. The newsman said a PAD (NASA voice update) announcement indicated something might have happened aboard *Apollo 13*. That was all — no specifics and nothing to indicate anything serious had occurred. Parrott was disturbed and called KPRC-TV to see if anyone had information. The station had none. Then he contacted the NBC office at Clear Lake Center. There was nothing there, either.

Next Parrott called the PAD office, where he learned the Apollo crew had reported some problem, with no details, and that the ground crew and the MSC had no confirmation. That was enough for Parrott and his friends. They weren't about to just sit and wait. Parrott remembered:

> John Shives and I took off in my car; Tom [Karonika] took his wife home and headed out to NASA. We both drove about 100 miles per hour at times. I got out at the Nassau Bay Hotel, location of NBC's "Bubble" studio, and Shives went on to the CBS site. I met the NBC unit manager outside the coffee shop and told him what I had heard. He went up to John Chancellor's room (Chancellor was then one of the NBC correspondents covering space stories) to alert him. I went upstairs to the Bubble, turned on the equipment and contacted New York. I got color bars and tone on the line. The unit manager contacted Fred Rhinestein, the NBC director and sat down to shade [adjust] the cameras. Fred got in touch with audio engineer Skip Johnson and video engineer Mickey Palmer.
>
> John Chancellor went on the air before anyone else with details of the explosion of a power cell aboard *Apollo 13*. NBC scooped everyone, and we feel that we had a lot to do with it.

Parrott is right. It was a major scoop, and he and his friends were alert and informed enough to make it happen. The on-board accident forced the mission to abort. *Apollo 13* circled the moon and returned to earth to splash down in the Pacific, where it was greeted by another eighteen-man KPRC-TV crew aboard the aircraft carrier *Iwo Jima*.

The remainder of the Apollo lunar flights went without serious problems, ending with *Apollo 17* in December 1972. NASA had further plans for the Apollo spacecraft, however. On May 14, 1973, a laboratory called *Skylab* was launched, followed on May 25 by a modified Apollo command module. After a linkup in earth orbit, the three-man crew spent the better part of a month in the laboratory, carrying out a long series of experiments. There were three more flights to *Skylab,* and for the final one, in the winter of 1973–74, the crew stayed in space almost two months.

There was one last hurrah for the Apollo series. On July 15, 1975, Tom Stafford, Vance Brand, and Donald K. "Deke" Slayton were launched into space for the first joining in orbit between a spacecraft of the United States and the Soviet Union's *Soyuz* spacecraft. Slayton was one of the original seven astronauts, barred from flight status until this mission because of a heart irregularity. Stafford had been commander of *Apollo 10.* Soviet cosmonauts Aleskey Leonov and Valeriy Kubasov were both veterans of the Russian program.

As usual, we were deeply involved in network coverage, but this time we added a new client. Moscow Television sent a crew to Houston, and we were to originate their reports to the Soviet Union. This brief association had its moments of special interest. The Russians had brought with them equipment designed to operate on the European standard of 220 volts. They had to buy some replacement parts locally, and we always wondered what the KGB thought about that. Because of the time differential, Moscow feeds went through in the hours long after midnight, but that was a minor inconvenience.

During the Apollo-Soyuz mission, the Soviet newsmen were obviously delighted with the freedom to talk with anyone they wanted to interview, and to photograph anything they wanted to photograph. The Russians even had plenty of free time to interview a number of Channel 2 staff people. But they seemed to be carefully avoiding talking with or photographing Bruce Bryant, who had been assigned to direct their postmidnight feeds to Moscow.

Bruce, a friendly, nice-looking young man who wore a neat mustache, beard, and long, carefully ordered hair, finally became curious. When he confronted one of the Russians and asked why they were shooting around him, the Russian denied it. Bruce persisted, and the Russian newsman conceded: "Because you look like Jesus Christ."

The Russians, citizens of an officially atheistic state, could not risk the disapproval of their superiors by transmitting a likeness which might remind viewers of the religious freedom they were denied.

From the beginning of America's space program, the vehicles had been designed for one-time use only and afterward became museum exhibits and laboratory specimens for researchers. It was the dream of NASA engineers to design and put into service a reusable spacecraft which could perform useful work in orbit, then return to earth for refitting. All this, of course, would lead eventually to the assembly of a space station and keep it supplied with all things necessary for long-term use.

The first flight of the shuttle vehicle named *Columbia* took place in April 1981, almost six years after the Apollo-Soyuz mission. *Columbia* was launched from Cape Canaveral, was controlled by Houston, and the vehicle, looking much like a conventional airplane, landed at Edwards Air Force Base in California. Our role was much the same as it had been throughout Gemini, Apollo, and Skylab. We provided manpower and facilities for network pool broadcasts and for exclusive NBC originations from Clear Lake.

Columbia flew once more in 1981 and three times in 1982. The first of that series ended at White Sands Missile Range in New Mexico, and the last put a communications satellite in orbit during the first operational trip of a shuttle. Then came the maiden flight of *Challenger*, in April 1983. *Challenger* flew twice more that year, both times landing at Edwards AFB after being "waved off" once from Kennedy Space Center because of bad weather. *Columbia* also flew in 1983 and then was put in storage until 1986.

Challenger's first 1984 flight was the first to end at Kennedy Space Center, where it had begun. The vehicle made two more trips that year, the last also ending in Florida. Aboard that mission was the first astronaut from another country, Marc Garneau of Canada. Between the second and third *Challenger* flights was the maiden mission of *Discovery*, the third ship in the shuttle fleet, and it made the last flight of the year, also ending at Kennedy. NASA was pleased. Crews had flown five times and retrieved two satellites which had gone astray after being launched.

In 1985 nine flights were launched and landed successfully: four by *Discovery*, three by *Challenger*, and two by the new shuttle, *Atlantis*. The passenger list was expanded to include the first member of Congress, Senator E. J. "Jake" Garn, on *Discovery*. A total of six foreign nationals crewed on other flights during the year as NASA stepped up its effort to maintain public interest in a program which was so successful it had become routine.

Nineteen eighty-six began quietly with the return to service of the veteran *Columbia*, and on January 12, another congressman, Representative Bill Nelson, flew the mission. Only six days later, January 18, *Challenger* was launched for what would have been its tenth flight and the beginning of its twenty-three millionth mile of travel through space. One minute and thirteen seconds into the launch, a rocket exploded. The orbiter and its crew of five men and two women were lost. As all the world knew, one was the teacher in space, Christa McAuliffe.

The emotional impact of such tragedy is impossible to measure, but many Channel 2 people, who had worked closely with NASA personnel for more than twenty years and who had come to know, respect, and admire them as human beings as well as dedicated professionals, felt the loss almost as deeply as the Clear Lake "family."

We will continue to be a proud part of America's continuing exploration of space. It will not be quite the same, though, ever again.

Moving On

PAUL HUHNDORFF

In the 1950s the KPRC stations were out beyond the suburbs. To the south and west was open prairie, with truck farms here and there. The few streets, including Post Oak Road, Westheimer, and Richmond, were two-lane blacktop. In the distance was the "city" of Bellaire, out at the far end of Bellaire Boulevard, another two-lane blacktop road.

At the southwest corner of Post Oak and Westheimer was a one-story brick school building no longer in use as a school. The old building had served during World War II as a Civil Defense headquarters. We had no near neighbors or shopping areas or restaurants, so we had our own cafeteria-style coffee shop providing regular meals under the watchful eye of Zenobia. Most of the land around us was owned by "old man" Voss, who himself mowed our grass. And the city of Houston's sewer system was nowhere near, so we had our own septic tank system out behind the carpenter shop.

From Post Oak, we watched the city grow right by us. During nineteen years we saw freeways built and watched the tremendous shopping and business complex called the Galleria take shape around the intersection of Post Oak and Westheimer. The little outdoor movie theater just north of us disappeared under a Galleria parking lot. The old school building made way for Neiman-Marcus, and we eventually got city sewer service. Finally, we were completely surrounded by a vibrant metropolis, and found we had outgrown what once had been the most modern television plant in the country. It was time to move again.

We wanted to stay in the southwest part of the city, partly because most of our staff lived in that area. We also needed immediate access to a major thoroughfare, so a location along the Southwest Freeway seemed the best choice. We studied several plots but found most to be too small for our purposes. Finally, we selected the site now designated 8181 Southwest Freeway. It had been owned by Houston Baptist College, but the administrators of the school decided they would never expand the campus that far west.

Once again, the KPRC stations were far out in the country, surrounded by vacant land, but this time we were on a freeway. We knew, from previous experience, it would be only a matter of time before the city would grow out to us again. Our architects, the same firm which had designed the new *Houston Post* building at Loop 610 and the Southwest Freeway, set to work. After several months, they presented a scale model of a broadcasting plant like none of us had ever seen before. We marveled at its vast expanses of glass and white concrete, and at the sheer volume of space contained within its walls.

As the building began to take shape, we and the contractor did have some concerns when the huge pit being excavated for the radio operation filled with water almost as rapidly as earth was removed. The problem was solved with drains and pumps. Among the several construction innovations was a method of building the triangular tower in front of the facility that would support microwave dishes and the radar antenna. Concrete was poured continuously, without seams, by hoisting the forms to keep up with the rising level of semi-liquid concrete within.

In order to reduce vibration from freeway traffic and various outside causes, each of the three television studios was literally suspended within the building, separated by corridors that also served as traffic ways. Acoustical treatment for the studios was designed by Dr. Paul Boner of the Physics Department of The University of Texas. Dr. Boner had also designed NBC's famous Studio 8H in Radio City that was the home of the great NBC Symphony Orchestra and its maestro, Arturo Toscanini, in radio's salad days.

Our new building was ready for occupancy in March 1972, and this time the move was accomplished at a more sedate pace. When we closed the Post Oak Road location, the new facility took over without interruption, so there was no midnight race. And the new plant lived up to expectations, although for weeks some of us had to pinch ourselves. Perhaps some of us still do.

We have changed transmitter locations and antenna towers even more frequently than we have studios. Our first transmitter and the 500-foot iron tower were right beside the first Post Oak quonset hut. Together, the transmitter and antenna produced an effective radiated power of 15 kilowatts for the visual signal and 7.5 kilowatts for the aural signal. When the studios and offices were moved in March 1953, the transmitter remained behind, but the following month we increased effective radiated visual power to 65 kilowatts.

We then began construction of a tower and antenna system adjacent to the new building at 3014 Post Oak Road. This gave KPRC-TV an effective visual power of 100 kilowatts, the maximum permitted a low-band station. This new tower extended Channel 2's coverage area by a radius of ten miles.

The new transmitter had to be transferred from the old location to the new building, which called for another overnight journey in order to lose no more broadcast time than necessary. We rehearsed for several nights before the scheduled move. After sign-offs, we disconnected the transmitter then reconnected to get an accurate time estimate and eliminate bugs in our procedure. The move was completed without incident on August 3, 1953, and we were finally all together in our first new home.

Newer stations coming on the air, both in our area and elsewhere, were able to take advantage of antenna advances from the beginning of their operations. We were aware that our signal, although at the maximum permitted under FCC rules, was not sufficient at some points near its perimeter to overcome local interference from electronic equipment and other sources. The best answer was to increase tower height and employ the latest antenna design. We started a search for a new transmitter site where we could erect a tower of at least 1,500 feet. A structure that high required approval from the Federal Aviation Authority. An acceptable site was found in an old oil development area called Blue Ridge, some four miles east of DeWalt and about twenty miles southwest of downtown Houston.

Together with the owners of KHOU-TV, we formed the Blue Ridge Tower Corporation and began construction of a tower to reach 1,549 feet above mean sea level. The tower would support at its top a triangular platform measuring 100 feet between its points. The design was called a "Candelabra" by Dresser-Ideco, the construction contractor. At one of the points we would install a six-bay GE TV-50-F antenna, actually two stacked three-bay antennas, to give us redundancy in case of failure of one of the elements. At another, KHOU-TV would install its antenna. And at the third, the tower company leased space to KHTV (TV) for its UHF antenna.

Each station would build its own transmitter building on site. In ours, we would install a GE TF3A amplifier and two GE TT-10A drivers, the second to serve as a backup should the first driver fail. Construction began February 12, 1964, and the complicated job was managed with only one mishap, which could have been serious. While one of the supporting cables was being hoisted into place, the tackle snapped and the cable fell into a tangle of steel wires. The cable itself "unlaid," completely ruined, and such cables are not "shelf" items. A new one had to be fabricated before the project could be completed. Miraculously, no one was injured.

On August 13, 1964, six months after construction started, KPRC-TV went on the air from the new transmitter and a tower spectacular enough to cause comment by motorists driving along any of the major U.S. and state highways that passed very near the site. Some concern was expressed by private pilots because, on misty days, the platform loomed above low-hanging clouds.

On one occasion a foolhardy pilot deliberately flew beneath one of the supporting cables, between the cable and the tower, without striking either. He was courting disaster. Not only would it have cost him his life had he struck either the tower or the cable, but it could have brought the entire structure down upon the cluster of buildings below, dealing death or injury to a number of others, and taking all three stations off the air, perhaps for months.

Houston area television viewers received a much clearer picture from the new antenna, especially in the fringe areas, and for more than fifteen years we made no major changes in our transmitter or tower.

In January 1979, during a period of severe cold weather, Wally Borries, working for an outside maintenance contractor, started up the Blue Ridge tower to service the two-way communications equipment mounted there. The elevator cable iced and the elevator car began to slip. Borries applied the emergency brake, got out, and climbed the remaining hundred feet to the top of the tower. Transmitter operators called a local steeplejack company, which sent two servicemen to free the elevator. They failed.

Suddenly there were three men marooned high above ground. In the meantime, the wind increased and was whistling through the skeleton of steel at fifty to sixty miles an hour. Predictions called for an overnight temperature drop to about twenty degrees. In desperation, a call went out to the U.S. Coast Guard Rescue Service. Soon a helicopter appeared over the tower and a basket was lowered. Despite driving wind and cold, all three men were safely rescued. The pilot of the helicopter, Lt. (j.g.) C. C. Rogers, received a well-deserved citation for his daring and successful performance.

In June of that year, in order to take advantage of substantial advances in electronic design and improve our picture quality at the receiver, we replaced our transmitters with two Harris Corporation BT25L2 units, again attaining state-of-the-art.

After more than seventeen years at Blue Ridge, the constant desire to further improve our signal and increase our range led us to begin searching for a site where we could once again increase the height of our antenna. Without question, one factor in our consideration was competitive pressure. KTRK-TV, after about the same number of years of operation from a tower nearby but somewhat lower than ours at Blue Ridge, announced plans to erect a tower in the 2,000-foot range some two miles to the northeast. Our problem was to find a location where the FAA would permit us to build a comparable facility. A site was found and approved in the same general area as the proposed KTRK-TV tower, and we invited the new owners of KHOU-TV, our partners in the Blue Ridge Corporation, to join in this venture. When Channel 11 declined, we entered into a joint ownership arrangement with KHTV(TV), the UHF station that had leased antenna space from the Blue Ridge Tower Corporation.

KTRK-TV management objected to our proposed location, claiming the possibility of interference between the two towers, although engineering studies had concluded no such interference would occur. Finally, after a delay of about a year, the FCC ruled in our favor and on December 15, 1983, construction started on a tower 2,049 feet above mean sea level.

Sixteen months later, on April 20, 1985, we began transmitting from an RCA TDM7A circular polarized antenna, located on a "Star Mount" atop the new tower, without interfering with our neighbors.

The most notable result of this new system was a much better picture on TV sets, especially those using rabbit-ear antennas.

From the first days, Channel 2 has maintained state-of-the-art ability to originate live sight and sound from any location within microwave range of our studios through the use of a fully equipped mobile remote unit. Neither of the other two network-affiliated stations in Houston has such equipment. Only KHTV (TV), the UHF independent station, has seen fit to make the required investment.

Those TV news vans called ENG units, with the small antennas mounted on top, aren't in the same league. They are designed to cover breaking news and do not include a control room or other production facilities for multiple camera originations.

In 1979, supported by KPRC-TV's long track record of successful and often profitable remote assignments, and with knowledge of the rapid advancements being made in remote equipment, I requested authority to build a new state-of-the-art mobile unit, and the matter came before a capital expenditures meeting that November. The cost of building the new system would be high, but I believed the expense could be recouped within a reasonable length of time. I projected three years. After some discussion, the subject was put aside, but near the end of the meeting, Bill Hobby raised it again, saying in effect, "If this unit can make money, why not proceed with it?"

With Bill Hobby's support, the project was approved, but Mrs. Hobby smilingly admonished us that she was going to hold the lieutenant governor and me personally responsible if it didn't pay for itself.

The new vehicle was ready for service in July 1980. We purchased five Ampex one-inch color cameras, for both studio and remote unit use. A year later we bought four more, giving us a total of nine cameras. Three of these are permanently assigned to the remote unit. Two and a half years after the meeting at which the unit was approved, I was able to report it had indeed paid for itself. Bill Hobby responded, "Paul, I'm glad. You saved both our lives."

Today, KPRC-TV is researching the latest proposals for state-of-the-art. When these ideas and drawings are ready to go on-line, we'll probably have our order placed and be waiting for delivery.

To Broader Horizons

JACK HARRIS

The buying and selling of television stations, frequently involving people and organizations not normally connected with broadcasting, and often at fantastic prices, has become a pattern in the eighties. It requires some effort to recall earlier times when our business proceeded at a much more modest pace and the faces were familiar. Of course, a certain amount of buying and selling has gone on almost from the very beginning. After all, we entered television broadcasting by "buying" Channel 2.

During the first twenty-five years of the operation of KPRC-TV, a sizable number of station sales had taken place as original owners retired or began thinking of putting their estates in order. From time to time, I had been made aware of opportunities to expand into other markets, but it had been the policy of our company to confine our interests to Houston.

In early 1975, Harte-Hanks Newspapers of San Antonio announced it had contracted to acquire Channel 12 in Jacksonville, Florida. At one of our regular weekly meetings, Mrs. Hobby remarked that she thought the Harte-Hanks group made a good buy, and wished she had known about the availability of the station. I replied that I had known the station was on the market, but had no idea our company would be interested in acquiring more properties. Mrs. Hobby indicated she would be interested in hearing about good prospects.

I knew of a possible opportunity. A station might be available in a market considerably larger than Jacksonville. I told her I had

118

reason to believe the owners of the CBS affiliate in Nashville, Tennessee, while not openly offering their station for sale, might consider selling if properly approached. Mrs. Hobby was quite interested.

The president and part owner of WLAC-TV was Tom Baker, who had been a high school and college classmate of mine, and who had been my friendly competitor when he became sales manager of Nashville's WLAC Radio and I was assistant manager of WSM Radio. I learned Baker could indeed be enticed, but was anxious that a possible sale of the station not be generally known. In fact, the visits I and others made to Nashville during negotiations had to be circumspect, cloaked in all kinds of subterfuge.

Baker and a business partner owned fifty percent of the station. The other fifty percent was held by American General Insurance Company of Houston, an interest acquired when American General had purchased Life and Casualty Insurance Company of Nashville. This fact became an immediate plus for us, because the principal officers of American General had the highest regard for the Hobby family and for their Houston broadcast properties. It became even more significant when I learned Baker was also talking with Harte-Hanks.

Bill Hobby and I paid a clandestine visit to Nashville, toured the station and analyzed the market. Then Houston Post Company vice-president and general counsel, Jim Crowther, secretary-treasurer Dan Thornburg, Jack McGrew, and Paul Huhndorff secretly visited to inspect the facilities. With Mrs. Hobby's approval, negotiations proceeded quickly and were completed successfully by Crowther. I learned later that the Harte-Hanks management was somewhat upset. They thought they had an inside track.

As it turned out, we bought Channel 5 in Nashville just before prices being offered and paid for television stations began to escalate sharply. Shortly afterward, a network affiliate in Oklahoma City, a less desirable market than Nashville, sold for about twice what we had paid. Because Channel 5's old call letters had been shared with WLAC Radio, which wished to retain them, we changed the Nashville television station's call to WTVF (TV), the "V" to remind the audience of the Roman numeral five.

Our next two acquisitions came from contacts by friends in the business. In the case of WTOK-TV, in Meridian, Mississippi, the president and part owner, Robert Wright, had turned over the assignment of finding a buyer to Clyde Haehnle, an officer in the station brokerage firm of R. C. Crisler and Company. Haehnle told me two potential buyers had already been located, but that both had been turned down by Wright, who wanted an owner imbued with a public conscience. Wright specifically mentioned our company as an example. I told Haehnle I doubted we would be interested, but I would check.

As it turned out, we were interested. Bill Hobby, Jim Crowther, and I visited the station. The price being asked was right, and we found Meridian to be a small but good market (the 181st in size in the country). In July 1981 the FCC approved our purchase of Channel 11, Meridian, and it became our third television property.

Less than a year later we were again approached by a friend, Don Diamond, a wealthy entrepreneur and owner of KVOA-TV, Channel 4, in Tucson, Arizona. Diamond had purchased the station in 1972 from Pulitzer Publishing of St. Louis, when the latter bought a Tucson newspaper and was required by FCC rules to divest itself of the television station. Now that he'd decided to sell, he elected to approach us first, so Bill Hobby, Jim Crowther, and I flew to Tucson. Both the station and the market were attractive. Hobby asked Diamond why he wanted to sell. Diamond replied that he believed the industry was rapidly being taken over by group owners, and individually owned stations would have difficulty competing in the future.

All three of us felt the station was well run under the management of Jon Ruby, and represented a good buy at a fair price. Crowther again worked out details, and at the end of June 1982, we assumed operation of KVOA-TV.

As the eighties wore on, Diamond's concerns about the future of stand-alone television stations appeared to be justified. Station groups became larger and more numerous, and the whole process accelerated in 1986, when the FCC more than doubled the number of stations one group could own. The FCC imposed only a cover on the aggregate number of total households one entity could serve, fixing it at twenty-five percent of the country's total. Our own situation changed too.

In December 1983, the *Houston Post,* long the anchor of the newspaper-radio-television complex, was sold. From that time forward, our focus would be on broadcast communications, and we geared ourselves internally for this new point of view. Each newly acquired station had become a subsidiary of Channel 2 Television Company, which in turn was a subsidiary of The Houston Post Company. Now all stations would become subsidiaries of H & C Communications, Inc. And H & C Communications would actively pursue opportunities for further expansion in broadcasting.

A list of markets seeming to offer unusual promise was put together, and a careful watch was set up to alert us when a desirable television station in any of those markets might be available. Meantime, large investment houses had become involved in the buying and selling process in order to finance purchases now running into hundreds of millions of dollars.

Howard Stark, a station broker, advised us early in 1984 that he had been invited to solicit bids for the ABC affiliate in Orlando, Florida, WFTV. Stark proposed that he represent H & C for a fee, and he would seek first refusal for us on the Orlando station. We agreed and began an intense study of the area. But even before Stark was able to meet with the principals of the operating company, the head of a group calling itself SFN Communications offered them, in effect, a blank check: "Name your price; we'll pay." The deal was concluded on the spot. A couple of years later, SFN Communications sold the station again for a tidy profit.

We were disappointed, of course, but our study of Orlando sharpened our interest. We noted that the principal stockholder of Cowles Broadcasting, Inc., owner and operator of the NBC affiliate in Daytona Beach–Orlando (and of the CBS affiliate in Des Moines, Iowa), was at a stage in life when he probably would be seriously concerned with estate problems and might be receptive to an offer for his company.

A letter extending an offer was sent to Cowles. Shortly thereafter, we were advised that Cowles Broadcasting had appointed a New York investment firm to solicit sealed bids. There were a number of bidders, but ours was accepted, and we began preparation of the assignment application which would transfer WESH-TV, Daytona Beach–Orlando, and KCCI-TV, Des Moines, to H & C. At that time, FCC rules still permitted no more than five VHF stations under the same ownership, so it became necessary to divest ourselves of one station. We elected to sell WTOK-TV in Meridian, since it was our smallest market.

With the completion of these transfers in January 1985, H & C became one of the larger group broadcasters in the country, and had done it within a span of about ten years.

In 1986 we learned the Rockefeller family had decided to sell all their broadcast properties operated through a subsidiary, Outlet Communications. Included in the list were network television affiliates in Orlando, Sacramento, and San Antonio. We could not purchase Orlando because of FCC rules against two-station ownership in any one market, but Outlet urged us to consider Sacramento. We looked at both the San Antonio and Sacramento markets, and finally decided on KSAT-TV, San Antonio, partly because it would give H & C another Texas station.

By the time the purchase of San Antonio's Channel 12 had been completed in August of 1986, the FCC ownership limit of five stations had been lifted. H & C Communications now owned six VHF network affiliates. Three were NBC affiliates (KPRC-TV, WESH-TV, and KVOA-TV); two were CBS (WTVF(TV) and KCCI-TV); and one was ABC (KSAT-TV). Through these stations, H & C serves well over five million television households in seven states.

Careful or You'll Get What You Ask For

JACK McGREW

The FCC imposed a licensing freeze in 1950 which lasted until July 1, 1952. No new stations went on the air, in the Houston area or elsewhere, until 1953. Our first competitor for television audience and advertisers' dollars was KGUL-TV, now KHOU-TV. Originally licensed to Galveston, the principal studios were in that city, but the transmitter and tower were at Hitchcock, much closer to Houston.

KGUL-TV signed on the air March 22, 1953, and affiliated with CBS. This meant KPRC-TV, beginning with the 1953 fall season, would no longer broadcast CBS programming. We were allowed, until that fall, to offer the best of CBS, including Jack Benny and Arthur Godfrey. Our affiliation with NBC, and KGUL-TV's with CBS, left ABC without a Houston market station, so top ABC shows were split between us.

The Kentucky Derby, then carried by CBS, was scheduled about five weeks after KGUL-TV began broadcasting. KGUL-TV wanted that show badly. We had already been ordered for it, but they tried anyway and finally got permission from CBS to carry it, but without network compensation. Thus, we both offered the big race, live, right in the middle of the ARB (American Research Bureau) May ratings sweep. When the rating books were released a few weeks later, KPRC-TV had a share of 99 for the event; KGUL-TV had 01. Since there would not be another rating book for Houston until the following November, KGUL-TV went into the fall selling season severely handicapped, to borrow a familiar horse-track expression.

When the FCC lifted its freeze on station licensing in July 1952, it also published a new table of channel allocations for the entire country. Houston was assigned two commercial channels and one educational VHF (Very High Frequency) channel, and Galveston was given one commercial. KPRC-TV had one of the two commercial Houston channels, of course, and KGUL-TV had the Galveston permit. The educational channel, 8, would eventually be licensed to the University of Houston and the Houston Independent School District (HISD), and would become the first educational station in the country.

Even though the university and the public school system shared the television license, only the university was really active in providing programming for the station. HISD's only real contribution was to pay $300 each month to have the school board meetings telecast.

The university found itself with only fifty percent ownership but with almost all of the expense of operating the facility and producing the programming. After two years of this relationship, the station's license was up for renewal and the University of Houston was unwilling to renew such a one-sided arrangement. The television station was recognized as a valuable asset, so the university made several pleas for the school board to shoulder more of the cost and provide more of the programming.

In a meeting with Channel 2's Jack Harris, the university officers pointed out that even if they were willing to continue to pay most of the cost and produce most of the programming, the fifty percent ownership by the school district made it possible, if not probable, that university programming could be pre-empted at any time HISD decided it wanted to go on the air. Under these circumstances, U of H officials simply weren't willing to even attempt long-term programming or any detailed expansion or modernization planning.

Harris recommended an application be filed to make the University of Houston sole licensee. In effect, this put the university and the school district into competition for Channel 8. The school board decided not to compete, and KUHT-TV became a part of the University of Houston system.

In 1955, only three years after the channel allocation table was published, the FCC announced it would consider two proposals: One would change all television grants in the country to the UHF (Ultra High Frequency) part of the spectrum; the other would change half the country to UHF, leaving the other half to VHF.

Consternation swept the industry. The first proposal would require major capital expenditures for every operating station. The second would create the same problem for at least half the stations. Either would disorient the entire system for broadcasters and viewers alike, and make obsolete millions of television receivers not equipped for UHF reception. It was in this grim atmosphere that about two dozen broadcasters met in New Orleans, in early 1956, to plan ways of combating this threat. KPRC-TV had taken a leading role in calling the meeting. General manager Jack Harris was named president of the organization which emerged: the Association of Maximum Service Telecasters (AMST).

Since that day, this organization has stood guard against government and private efforts to degrade the spectrum upon which television depends for its very life. In the mid-1960s, it was the AMST (later abbreviated MST) which proposed and pushed through Congress the "all channel" legislation, requiring that all sets manufactured in the future be capable of receiving both VHF and UHF signals, without a converter. This legislation permitted operators of UHF stations to become competitive in the marketplace and reduced pressure to squeeze in hundreds of additional VHF channels, which would have hurt reception. The result was the highly competitive television system we enjoy today.

Incidentally, Harris was MST's president for sixteen years, and H & C Communications still maintains its close relationship with this important trade organization through Henry Catto, who serves on its board of directors and several of its committees.

Scattershots

*A collection of anecdotes and reminiscences about people, places,
and events as contributed by several authors*

HEAD 'EM UP AND MOVE 'EM OUT

The "Salt Grass Trail," long a hallowed Houston tradition
that makes the Houston Livestock Show and Rodeo unique, originated as a KPRC-TV project. The story began in the Cork Club,
the showplace of Glenn McCarthy's Shamrock Hotel, where Jack
Harris was meeting with Charlie Giezendanner, partner in the advertising agency representing the stock show. Reese Lockett, per-
ennial mayor of Brenham and longtime grand marshal of the opening night parade, was also on hand. They were trying to devise new
promotional ideas for that year's edition of the show when the discussion was interrupted by Clark Nealon, then sports editor of the
Houston Post.

Their conversation turned to the last time Nealon and Lockett
had been together. Both men had been grounded by bad weather in
Miami, following the Orange Bowl game. Lockett had sworn he
would never again get any farther from Brenham than he could ride
on a horse. He reminisced that he and his father, and assorted other
male relatives, used to drive their cattle to market in Houston along
the old Salt Grass Trail, roughly following the course of today's
U.S. Highway 290.

Inspiration struck, and despite a little occasional quibbling,
credit for the idea is generally conceded to Harris. Why not revive
the Salt Grass Trail, and use it as a centerpiece for promoting the
stock show? The project immediately began to take shape. The trail

riders, friends, and neighbors of Lockett would assemble at Lockett's place near Brenham. They would have an evening of fun together, then early next morning set off by horse and covered wagon for Houston. The trip was expected to take a couple of days. Lockett would be trail boss, and Harris volunteered the services of Pat Flaherty, KPRC-TV's first news director, as wagon boss. Harris also promised all-out coverage by the only television station in town.

Planners didn't seriously intend for the riders to make the trip all the way from Brenham on horseback. The start would be legitimate enough through the city of Brenham, but once well out of town, the party would be met by a discreet caravan of trailers. They would load their horses, the erstwhile riders would enter limousines, and the entire group would proceed to the outskirts of Chappell Hill. There the riders would again mount for a parade through town. Once past Chappell Hill, the procedure would be repeated at Hempstead, Waller, and so on.

The plan was enthusiastically adopted, and the promotion began. On the appointed day, invited riders assembled outside Brenham and bedded down for the night. So much for the plan. When they awoke next morning they were greeted by what seemed like hundreds of volunteer trail riders, already saddled up and ready to go. There was no escape. Every miserable foot of trail would have to be ridden in earnest. And Lockett claimed the weather was probably the worst he had seen since he was a boy. It was bitterly cold with enough wind to drive icy water through the toughest slicker and thickest longjohns. Rain soon turned to sleet. But most of the hardy pathfinders toughed it out.

The ride ended three days later at the original KPRC-TV studios behind Pin Oak stables. The big overhead doors into the studio were opened, and the first few riders, accompanied by Flaherty and his wagon, rode in. They were cold, wet, dirty, unshaven, sleepless, and triumphant.

The Salt Grass Trail became a permanent prelude to the Houston Livestock Show and has been widely copied around the country. Nowadays, of course, participants are fully aware of the obligation when signing on, and the event has become institutionalized, with rules and policies and procedures. Which is not to say that from time to time there is not a hint of the old, carefree ways. It's likely that the founding fathers, most of them now passed to their reward, would approve.

LEGAL EAGLE

An essential requisite to the operation of any successful business, and particularly if that business is engaged in communications, is a good lawyer. Our company was blessed for many years with one of the best.

The late Jack Binion was one of the senior partners of the law firm representing our organization for many years. The firm ranks among the most prestigious in the state and nation. Fortunately for us, Binion took a lively interest in the business of broadcasting and was our prime resource when we felt in need of counsel or comfort. No question was too unimportant for his personal attention, and his advice was always tempered by his practical approach.

He understood our business and appreciated the fact that we did take seriously our obligation to "serve the public interest, necessity, and convenience," even if doing so sometimes meant we had to choose the more difficult and hazardous route. He also gave us full credit for our responsible approach to our profession. His advice in a delicate situation was: "If you think you should do it, do it. I'll see that you don't go to jail."

On one occasion, the subject of a critical comment by one of our broadcasters threatened to sue us for libel. Binion smiled. "I hope he doesn't try it," he said. "But if he does, I can prove he's a thief."

Jack Binion fully supported our decision to challenge the Federal Communications Commission (FCC) in court, even though our Washington counsel considered the move risky. The suit grew out of our concern, shared by every other broadcast station in the country, for the probable consequences of the Port Huron decision. In that decision the FCC denied stations the right to censor or edit statements made by a candidate for public office, even though such statements might be libelous or otherwise defamatory in nature, and even though the station might then find itself a defendant in a lawsuit resulting from such statements. The dilemma was obvious, yet most broadcasters were reluctant to challenge the decision for fear of antagonizing the powerful federal agency that regulated the business.

Governor and Mrs. Hobby strongly believed candidates should be free of all censorship, but they were also acutely aware of the dangers involved. In our case, the matter was made more urgent by an approaching county contest involving two bitter rivals for the office of sheriff. Each was expected to make serious charges against the other. For our own protection, and to clarify the situation for the benefit of the industry, we decided to contest the decision.

The case was heard by a three-judge federal court in Houston. The FCC regarded the challenge as sufficiently serious to assign its general counsel to the hearing. We were represented by Jack Binion. Both Governor Hobby and Jack Harris were called to testify. Binion argued what seemed to us to be the clear incongruity of the decision: we had no right to edit remarks yet were liable for damages. He asked that the FCC be enjoined from enforcing its rule.

When the court's opinion was handed to Binion he turned to the last paragraph, which said our petition was denied. Disappointed, he called Harris and reported, "We lost." Minutes later, he called again, "Hold everything."

Finally, after a few more agonizing minutes, he reported, "We won!" The court found it inconceivable the FCC would deny a broadcast station the right to censor a candidate's remarks, even though the station would be responsible for any injury those remarks might cause. However, since no action had been taken against us by the FCC under the Port Huron rule, the court denied our request. On the other hand, the opinion added, should the court learn that the commission had taken such action, it would grant us an immediate injunction.

Thus, for the benefit of the entire broadcast industry, the FCC was put on notice not to attempt to enforce its Port Huron decision. Subsequently, the problem was resolved when Congress wrote into Section 315 of the Communications Act an express prohibition of censorship of remarks uttered by a candidate himself, and the Supreme Court ruled that Congress could not have intended to compel a licensee to broadcast libelous statements and at the same time subject that licensee to the risk of damage suits.

No matter was too far removed from the regular business of broadcasting to prompt Jack Binion to ignore it. On one occasion, a staff maintenance man died, and his insurance policy named his estranged wife, then living in California, as his beneficiary. With the collaboration of another woman, a mortuary owner planned an elaborate funeral which would have exhausted the proceeds of the policy. Binion made a telephone call to the mortuary owner, and the fancy funeral was dropped in favor of a perfectly suitable but considerably less expensive service.

Much more serious was the case of the high school age son of one of our employees. The boy had killed another youngster of about the same age with a random pistol shot during a midnight automobile chase through a state park. The district attorney's office, perhaps under pressure from the dead boy's parents and friends, was pressing for commitment to a state facility for juvenile offenders.

Binion, by his own admission, had not tried a criminal case since leaving East Texas as a young lawyer, but he put aside his other assignments and took personal charge. He spent hours driving through the park, trying to reconstruct events of the tragic night. He talked with each witness to the shooting.

When the case was called before the juvenile court judge, he stood with the boy before the bench. His argument persuaded the judge to place the youngster in the care of Cal Farley, operator of the famous Boys Ranch, who had already agreed to accept him as a resident if the court would permit.

Jack Binion never presented a bill for his services in the case.

COUNTRY GENTLEMAN

Harris County was a major farming and ranch area only a few years ago. Much of what is now the city of Houston was rice farms and fairly large (5,000-acre or so) cattle ranches. KPRC Radio had a regular morning farm and ranch show, and when The Houston Post Company bought Channel 2, the farm and ranch show moved over to television. George Roesner was the longtime host of the radio show, and he also made the move.

George was the archetypical Texas Aggie, described by the *Houston Post*'s Bill Bedell as a man who spoke "pure-dee Texas." Non-natives tended to wait for the translation when trying to carry on much of a conversation with George, but he had a loyal audience of early-rising farmers and ranchers. They, too, spoke "pure-dee Texas."

One morning George's guests on RFD-TV included a young woman who had won a 4-H Club scholarship. Her family had scraped together the money to send her off to school with a new wardrobe and had stopped off for the night at a Houston motel before delivering her to the schoolhouse door. During the night a thief had broken into the family car and stolen everything.

Another guest on that particular show was one of the area's better known "gentleman farmers," in real life a major building contractor. He sat, waiting his turn at the microphone, while George talked to the 4-H Clubber, then he talked about his brand of "farming" with George to wrap up the show.

As the guests said their off-camera goodbyes, the gentleman farmer shook hands with the heartbroken victim of the automobile burglar, then hurried away to another appointment. The young woman opened her hand to find a neatly folded thousand-dollar bill.

The government doesn't make thousand-dollar bills anymore, but Houston still turns out "quiet philanthropists."

George Roesner was always at odds with the people on the technical side at Channel 2. When he went into the field he wore a pair of heavy rubber boots, strapped a portable tape recorder around his neck, and operated, or attempted to operate, a spring-wound 16mm movie camera loaned to him by the news department. The tape recorder and the camera were in the repair shop on a regular basis.

George tended to treat both devices the same way he treated his rubber boots, tossing them into the trunk of his car when he was through with them and washing them off when they became covered with the accumulated debris from a hundred rice fields and a thousand feed lots.

But Houston area farmers and ranchers embraced George and his "crack of dawn" television show. He knew what they were all about and he cared about their triumphs and troubles. His position in early Houston television was summed up by a co-worker, one of the station's camera operators, Bobby Parker. The gentle giant of a man with a dry sense of humor masked behind a pronounced stammer, stared into his camera viewfinder one morning and said, "Th-th-there's old G-George — a t-t-television m-man among f-f-farmers, and a f-f-farmer among t-television m-men."

BREAKOUT

Although it seems unlikely, our studios on Post Oak once became the scene of a prison escape. We had worked with the prison system for a number of years in a rehabilitation program for convicts who were about to be released, trying to help find them jobs on the outside. As part of that effort we used prison talent from time to time, usually on remote broadcasts from prison installations, but occasionally in our studios, and that led to the "breakout."

An inmate band was driven under guard from Huntsville. For security's sake, the inmate musicians were brought into the building through the prop room at the back and were directed into the main radio studio, where they were to rehearse. Not realizing there were doors at each end of the studio, the guards thought the prisoners would be secure. The convict musicians put down their instruments and walked straight out, through the adjacent coffee shop where several employees were taking a break. By the time the guards realized what had happened, their charges had disappeared into the cluster of buildings across Post Oak Road. It was several days before all were recaptured and returned to "the Walls." Needless to say, from then on, rules concerning excursions outside the prison were considerably tightened.

The *Houston Press,* a lively afternoon daily of the time, ran a banner headline: "KPRC-TV Station Break."

A KICK IN THE PANTS

In the mid-1980s the worldwide fall in petroleum prices was particularly hard on Houston. The boom days of ever-escalating oil revenues and ever-increasing demand were over, and Houston suffered a near knockout blow to the economic chin.

The effect on the "Golden Buckle of the Sunbelt" was emotional as well as economic. The city's self-image was badly bruised, and people were beginning to discount or overlook or reject even the positive elements that have kept Houston a vibrant city, during tough times as well as better times.

There was a sense of acceptance at work. People from all areas were beginning to believe the worst of the bad publicity, even in the face of contradictory facts.

Channel 2 decided that those "facts" needed reevaluating and that the positive side of things needed emphasis. Working with producer Bob Heller, the station designed a series of four documentary programs with the expressed purpose of boosting the city's self-image.

The titles indicated the scope and the purpose: "HOUSTON: On the Move Again," "HOUSTON: Dawning of a New Age," "HOUSTON: The Bountiful City," and "Leadership HOUSTON: Feast or Famine."

The four programs were promoted extensively for just what they were — a close look at all of the things that were right with the nation's fourth largest city. They were edited to emphasize that a problem recognized is a problem on the way to solution. The shows made the point that as bad as things were, they could be a lot worse and that there were many strengths being minimized or overlooked during the economic downturn.

Producer Heller and Channel 2 camera teams investigated the economy, both from where it stood and where it could be directed. The Houston lifestyle, considered by many citizens to be in serious decline, was compared with other major cities. And the comparison proved more than favorable.

Even transportation and Houston's reputation as a city with a hopelessly congested traffic problem were analyzed. Again, comparisons were made, both in the reality of the mid-1980s and in the planning for the future. Houston's METRO system and the long-range planning for city transportation were shown to be better than just good, in fact to be among the best of the nation's major cities.

Even with frank recognition of the problems, narrator Ron Stone was able to show conclusively during these four half-hour productions that Houston's plight was nowhere near as bad as it was being perceived.

Just as importantly, the four programs pointed out all of the ongoing and escalating efforts being made to combat the problems and the perceptions, and they revealed that progress was already being made.

When the first of the four shows went on the air, prospective sponsors weren't exactly standing in line to participate. But by the time the fourth show was scheduled, the sponsorships were sold out. The after-effect of the series was also gratifying. There were calls and letters from people in all walks of life, and all of them were positive. The Houston Chamber of Commerce and several of the area's major industries asked for and received copies of the programs for further viewing. METRO used the series as a part of its long-range planning and promotional efforts, making available to a wide audience the other side of the coin.

In the long run, the fact that the four programs ran as documentary specials on Channel 2 in evening hours was only the beginning of a very candid and very successful booster effort that benefited the entire community in a big way.

In Closing

TOM REIFF

I have two framed interoffice memos on my office wall. The first, dated March 15, 1951, directs the station's accounting department to add my name to the payroll. The job: camera operator. The salary: $200 per month. The man who hired me also assured me I would be able to work four overtime hours each week. I was thrilled.

The other memo is dated November 19, 1975. It announced my appointment to the station's board of directors. The twenty-four years between the memos allowed me to watch a young and struggling mass medium become, and remain, the dominant social force in this country. The hardware got smaller and better. I changed job categories several times: camera operator, floor manager, junior director (a title now mercifully deceased), director, low-octane comedy writer, local sales account executive, sales development director (I never really understood what that one meant), program director for both the radio and television stations. I also got a raise.

It occurred to me I had spent most of my life with this company. On the day of that happy realization, I didn't know whether to laugh or cry. It is, in some contemporary circles, a given that mobility is always vital and always upward, and any long-term relationship is closely related to one of the more undesirable social diseases.

KPRC-TV has enjoyed the benefit of being a family-owned business for almost forty years. Today we live in an environment of highly leveraged, bring-it-to-the-bottomline, increase-the-earnings-per-share mergers and buyouts. I think our value system, as an industry, has become warped. A company must, of course, make sound business decisions in order to prosper and grow. This company has worked toward that end, as well as working to serve. One of the primary reasons I never opted to leave the station is that the Hobby family has a long record of community commitment and service, and has established a standard which has been implemented by some talented, devoted, and dedicated people. I hope, someday, to be counted among them.

I have been privileged to be part of some wonderful fund-raising efforts. Probably the most satisfying was raising enough money to provide a fully equipped and paid-for facility for job training of the blind, and a school for blind youngsters. I was privileged to be there when television, quite possibly, held the nation together after President Kennedy was killed; when Wilma Mason Rudolph, who was so badly burned as a child she wasn't supposed to walk again, streaked across the finish line to earn the gold medal for the USA Women's 400 Meter Relay Team in Rome; when Alan Shepard and John Glenn and Neil Armstrong made us all stand a little taller; and when that sudden awful explosion made us lower our heads in grief as *Challenger* brought us back to the darker side of reality in our effort to fully develop the last frontier. We cheered together, and we cried together, when a tiny vulnerable girl in Midland was lifted from what could have been her dying place by hands accustomed to much rougher and less-loving work.

The pictures in our electronic album are poignant, funny, beautiful, conscience-raising, exhilarating, depressing, and most important, accurate benchmarks as to who we are, and who we are likely to be.

Ours is a time when privately held mass media companies outnumber confirmed unicorn sightings by only a handful. The unsettling part is that fewer and fewer voices will be heard in the media arena, and a disproportionate number of those voices will belong to those who know the price of everything and the value of nothing.

I lied to you before. Actually, I got a couple of raises.

The Writers

JACK HARRIS, consultant, H & C Communications, Inc. Retired, 1983, as president, Broadcast Division, H & C Communications, Inc. Entered radio in 1933 as part-time sports announcer at WSM and WLAC, Nashville, while undergraduate at Vanderbilt University. Joined WSM, 1935, organized special events department, and became director of news and special events. Joined War Department, 1941, as civilian assistant to special advisor on radio to secretary of war. During World War II served as second in command, radio section, War Department public relations; then as chief of radio and press communications for Gen. Douglas MacArthur. Handled radio and press arrangements for Japanese surrender ceremony. Discharged, 1946, as colonel, and returned to WSM as associate general manager. Joined KPRC Radio, 1947, as general manager. Became general manager of KPRC-TV, as well as KPRC Radio, 1950, when television was acquired. President, Channel 2 Television Company, KPRC Radio Company, Channel 5 Television Company (Nashville); vice-president and member, board of directors, The Houston Post Company. Served on NAB committees which organized Television Bureau of Advertising and Television Information Office, and was a founder and first president of Association of Maximum Service Telecasters. Former chairman of NBC-TV affiliates. Vice-president and member of board of Muscular Dystrophy Association of America, member of board of Radio Free Europe/Radio Liberty, Texas Association of Developing Colleges, and United Negro College Fund. Member of advisory boards: the United States Armed Services, the U.S. Navy, U.S. Information Service, Voice of America, Executive Reserve, School of Communications of The University of Texas and of the University of Houston. Among his awards and honors: NAB Distinguished

137

Service Award, 1979; Honorary Ph.D., Wiley College; honoree of "Jack Harris Research Unit," Baylor College of Medicine; "Torch of Liberty" Award of Anti-Defamation League, B'nai B'rith.

*   *   *

JACK McGREW, consultant, H & C Communications, Inc. Retired, 1981, as executive vice-president, Channel 2 Television Company, and station manager, KPRC-TV. Entered radio, 1930, as announcer, KFDM, Beaumont. Joined KPRC Radio, 1936, as announcer. Named program director, 1937. Organized KPRC Radio news department, 1940. Named assistant manager, KPRC Radio, 1947. Station manager and sales manager, KPRC and KPRC-TV, 1953. Board member of The Houston Post Company, Channel 2 Television Company, and Channel 5 Television Company, Nashville. Chairman of board of Television Bureau of Advertising, 1973.

*   *   *

PAUL HUHNDORFF, director of engineering, Broadcast Group, H & C Communications, Inc. Graduate of Port Arthur Radio College. Entered radio, 1938, as engineer for KTRH Radio. 1942, installed communications equipment in C-1 cargo vessels at Bethlehem Steel shipyards, Beaumont. Joined U.S. Army Signal Corps, 1943, and reached rank of sergeant. Engineer, KTHT Radio, 1946, and helped build KOPY-FM, first frequency modulation (FM) station in Texas. Joined KLEE Radio, 1947, as chief engineer. Named chief engineer, KLEE-TV, 1948, and supervised construction of station. Has served as vice-president and operations manager, Channel 2 Television Company; board member, Channel 2 Television Company; vice-president, Blue Ridge Tower Corporation. Life senior member, Institute of Electrical and Electronics Engineers; member, Society of Motion Picture and Television Engineers; past president, Bellaire Kiwanis Club; and past president, Bellaire's Faith Lutheran Church.

*   *   *

THOMAS H. REIFF, president and general manager, Channel 2 Television Company. Graduate of University of Houston with B.S., radio/television. Entered television as cameraman, KPRC-TV, 1951. Has served as director, account executive, program director, and vice-president of programming for KPRC-TV; program director, KPRC Radio; executive vice-president and general manager of

WESH-TV, Orlando; and board member of Channel 2 Television Company, Houston, and Channel 2 Television Company of Florida, Orlando. Industry memberships include Legislative Committee of NBC Affiliates, National Association of Television Program Executives, National Association of Broadcasters, and board of directors of Texas Association of Broadcasters. Received University of Houston Distinguished Communications Alumnus Award, 1987.

* * *

JACK CATO, police reporter, Channel 2 News. Graduate of the University of Missouri's School of Journalism with extensive experience in both radio and television operation in Kansas City and Houston. Spent nine years as a stockbroker before returning to Channel 2 and his first love, television news, where he has spent the last twenty years.

* * *

PHIL ARCHER, senior reporter, Channel 2 News. Reporter for Houston News Service, 1976. Joined Channel 2 News, August 1976. William Benton Fellow in Broadcasting, University of Chicago, 1983–84. Returned to Channel 2 News, 1984. Winner of Pierenger Award, 1978; United Press International Best Series Award, 1983; Associated Press Best Documentary, 1983.

* * *

GARY JAMES (TIDWELL), executive producer, "The Eyes of Texas." Entered broadcasting as announcer-newsman at KBST, Big Spring, Texas, 1954. Served as newsman, KVET-TV, and as production manager, KHUT-FM, both Austin, 1958–60. Was also news writer-reporter-broadcaster, KLRU-TV, Austin PBS station, 1959–60; and news director, KRIC, Beaumont, 1960–61. Joined Channel 2 News, 1961. Held broadcast scholarship, University of Texas, 1958. Member of National Press Photographers Association. Winner of George Foster Peabody Award; NPPA Team Filming, General News, Feature, and Cameraman of the Year, Region Five Awards; Hollywood Film Festival Best Spot News Award; Regional Emmy of National Academy of Television Arts and Sciences (twice); Radio and Television News Directors Association, First Place Documentary Award; and State Bar Association First Place Documentary Award.

*   *   *

FRANK DOBBS, independent filmmaker, former Channel 2 News reporter, photographer, writer, producer, and assistant news director for special projects. Winner of the 1969 "News Film Cameraman of the Year" award from the National Press Photographers' Association. Recent independent productions include: "Houston, the Legend of Texas," CBS-TV three-hour "Special Event"; "Uphill all the Way," theatrical feature film; "Lone Star Bar and Grill," Showtime Cable System nine-hour mini-series; and "Hotwire," theatrical feature film. Also writer of several episodes of "Gunsmoke," CBS-TV prime-time series. Member of Directors Guild of America, Writers Guild of America-West, Motion Picture Producers of Texas, Informational Film Producers of America, International Quorum of Motion Picture Producers, and American Film Institute. Winner of Wrangler Trophy of National Western Heritage Center and Cowboy Hall of Fame; Blue Ribbon Award of the American Educational Film Festival; Best of Show Award of Oklahoma Film Festival; Best of Show Award of Milan Film Festival; Golden Eagle Award of the Council for Non-Theatrical Events (five times); Chris Statuette of the Columbus Film Festival (three times); Best Director Award of the Cartagena Film Festival; Cindy Award of the Informational Film Producers of America (twice); and a Special Jury Award for Writing from the Informational Film Producers of America.

*   *   *

LOIS FARFEL STARK, president, Stark Productions, Inc., producer/writer of documentary films. From 1967 to 1974 was producer, NBC Network News, for documentary programs: "NBC Reports," "First Tuesday," and "Chronolog." In addition to documentary films for KPRC-TV, has served as consultant to NBC News for "Labor in the Promised Land," "Just Plain Folks: The Hunts," and "Medicine in America: Life, Death, and Dollar"; and as field producer for NBC News for "The American Family." Member of American Women in Radio and Television, Texas Association of Film Tape Professionals, Houston Motion Picture Council, and American Film Institute. Trustee of St. John's School, Texas Children's Hospital, Sarah Lawrence College, and American Institute for Public Service; member of Rhodes Scholar Selection Committee, Texas Commission on the Arts-Media Panel, Board of Visitors of the University of Houston, and Texas Committee for the Humanities; director and former vice-president of Alley Theater; and director of American Jewish Committee. Winner of American Bar Association Silver Gavel Award, CINE Golden Eagle Award (twice), Second Place Award of Texas Association of Broadcasters, Jury Gold Award of the International Film Festival of the Americas, the Matrix Award of Women in Communications, and a nominee for National Academy of Television Arts and Sciences Emmy Award.

KPRC-TV News
Honors and Awards

Sigma Delta Chi Distinguished Service Award, Public Service in
Television Journalism, 1984
Alfred I. Dupont Columbia University Awards, Citation for Dis-
tinction, 1982–83
National Academy of Television Arts and Sciences:
Emmy Nomination: "Guns are for Killing," 1965–66
Emmy Nomination: "Are We Killing the Gulf?" 1970–71
National Press Photographers Association:
Newsfilm Station of the Year, 1963
Newsfilm Cameraman of the Year, 1969
First Place, Spot Newsfilm, 1972
First Place, Team Filming, 1972
Third Place, Feature, 1972
Honorable Mention, Children's Feature, 1972
Radio/Television News Directors Association:
Distinguished Achievement, On-the-spot News Story, 1972
Distinguished Achievement, Editorializing on Television,
1974
Distinguished Achievement, On-the-spot News Story, 1977
Distinguished Achievement, Investigative Reporting, 1986
United Press International, National Awards, Southwest Region:
First Place, Spot News, 1983
First Place, Documentary, 1983
First Place, Sports, 1983
UPI Broadcasters Association of Texas:
Best Feature, 1971–72
Best Newscast, 1972–73

Best Editorial, 1973–74
Best Spot News, 1973–74
Wendell Mayes Memorial Public Affairs Award, 1974–75
Best Investigative Reporting, 1981–82
First Place, News Series, 1983
First Place, Photojournalism, 1983
First Place, Spot News, 1983
First Place, Documentary Special, 1983
Outstanding Achievement, News Series, 1983
Outstanding Achievement, Feature, 1984
Outstanding Achievement, Investigative Reporting, 1984
Outstanding Achievement, Newscast, 1985
Texas Associated Press Broadcasters:
Best Feature, 1970
Extraordinary News Event, 1971
Best Series, First Place, Division 1, 1982
Best Reporter, First Place, Division 1, 1982
Best Reporter, First Place, Division 1, 1983
Best Photography by Station, First Place, Division 1, 1983
Best Investigative Report, First Place, Division 1, 1983
Texas Association of Broadcasters:
Merit Award, Editorial, 1973
Merit Award, Editorial, 1975
Merit Award, Investigative Reporting, 1984
Merit Award, Spot News, 1984
Merit Award, Spot News, 1986
Headliners Club:
Individual Achievement Award, Television Feature, 1981
Individual Achievement Award, Informative Reporting, 1987
NBC News Affiliate News Service:
Station of the Year, 1985
Station of the Year, 1986
State Bar of Texas Journalism Awards Competition, 1971–72
Republic of Texas Award, 1978

In Memoriam

Governor William P. Hobby

Fred Bradley
Fred Burton
Ted Carr
Jane Christopher
Earl Corridon
Jack Edmonds
Bill Enis
Pat Flaherty
"Texas Ruby" Fox
Nadine "Katy" Hammer
Kirt Harriss
Thomas Hill
Twinell "Skipper" Johnson
Bobby Lahr
Bruce Layer
Plush Lee

Ralph Mead
Gene Osborne
Bobby Parker
Fred Parks
Robert (Ed) Parsons
Bob Poole
Larry Rasco
Althea Sellers
Will Sinclair
Clifton Smith
Bill Starks
Dave Stickley
Preston Strader
Carl Sutton
Gary Wallace
Ray Wright

Chronology

January 21, 1948. The Houston Post Company, owner and operator of KPRC, files application for television station in Houston to be operated on Channel 4.

January 30, 1948. W. Albert Lee is granted construction permit for television station in Houston to be operated on Channel 2.

January 1, 1949. KLEE-TV begins service on Channel 2 at 9:30 P.M. after about 3¹/₂-hour delay caused by transmitter trouble. Number of television sets in market believed to be 2,000.

March 28, 1950. The Houston Post Company and W. Albert Lee file application for assignment of license of KLEE-TV to The Houston Post Company. Price is $743,000.

May 23, 1950. Application for assignment of license of KLEE-TV to The Houston Post Company granted.

June 1, 1950. The Houston Post Company assumes ownership and begins operation of KLEE-TV.

July 3, 1950. Call letters change from KLEE-TV to KPRC-TV. Three-day television trade fair and show begins at Plantation Club. Number of television sets in market believed to be 26,000.

July 22, 1950. Texas primary election returns are televised direct from the city room of the *Houston Post*.

September 30, 1950. First football game in new Rice Stadium — Rice versus Santa Clara — televised by Channel 2.

December 1950. Number of television sets in market estimated to be 53,750.

December 2, 1951. Houston Post estimates number of television sets in market to be 100,000.

July 1, 1952. Federal Communications Commission ends freeze on issuance of construction permits for new television stations.

July 7, 1952. KPRC-TV inaugurates live network service with coverage of Republican National Convention.

July 21, 1952. KPRC-TV carries live coverage of Democratic National Convention.

August 1952. KPRC-TV carries first live simultaneous telecast of regularly scheduled network programs.

September 1952. KPRC-TV carries live play-by-play coverage of baseball World Series.

March 20, 1953. KPRC-TV and KPRC move into new facility at 3014 Post Oak Road. Number of television sets in market estimated at 200,000.

March 22, 1953. KGUL-TV, later to become KHOU-TV, signs on, licensed to serve Galveston market on Channel 11.

April 1953. KPRC-TV increases power from 15,000 to 65,000 watts.

May 12, 1953. KUHT-TV, country's first educational television station, begins service in Houston on Channel 8.

August 1953. KPRC-TV begins service from new 749-foot tower and six-bay antenna at 3014 Post Oak Road; increases power to 100,000 watts, maximum for low-band VHF station.

September 14, 1953. London, England, resident claims to have received KLEE-TV call letters. Claim finally determined to be hoax.

October 20, 1953. KNUZ-TV, later to become KHTV, begins Houston's first UHF service (Channel 39).

December 21, 1953. FCC approves compatible color television standards.

March 1954. KPRC-TV buys its first radar unit, a war surplus fire control system from a U.S. battleship, and modifies it for use as a weather radar — the first in the area.

May 3, 1954. KPRC-TV carries its first color program, "Voice of Firestone," from NBC.

November 20, 1954. KTRK-TV begins service on Channel 13.

November 22, 1954. FCC grants KTRE-TV, Lufkin, satellite status to carry KPRC-TV programs.

April 17 and 19, 1955. KPRC-TV originates "Dinah Shore Show" from Shamrock Hotel for NBC.

October 30, 1955. KPRC-TV originates segment of "Wide Wide World" for NBC, featuring Houston Symphony Orchestra conducted by Leopold Stokowski.

October 1956. KPRC-TV originates segment of "Wide Wide World" for NBC from Huntsville Prison Rodeo.

November 25, 1956. KPRC-TV originates segment of "Wide Wide World" from Temple Emanu-El, narrated by Rabbi Robert I. Kahn.

February 3, 1957. KPRC-TV originates entire "Wide Wide World" for NBC, including pickups from San Jacinto Monument, the Battleship *Texas*, a helicopter circling over the Houston Ship Channel, and a shrimp boat in the Gulf of Mexico off Galveston.

February 25, 1958. KPRC-TV is first independently owned television station in Texas, and twelfth station in country, to take delivery on Ampex VR-1000 videotape recorder (first commercially practical tape unit).

January 18–23, 1960. KPRC-TV feeds "Queen for a Day" to NBC from City Auditorium for entire week.

March 6, 1960. KPRC-TV originates "Roy Rogers Show" for NBC from Houston Livestock Show.

September 5, 1960. KPRC-TV inaugurates "Midnight with Marietta," featuring Marietta Marich — perhaps first local late-night talk show in country.

September 1961. KPRC-TV covers Hurricane Carla; wins wide acclaim for coverage.

July 1964. KPRC-TV replaces its homemade weather radar antenna with M33 NIKE-Zeus tracking antenna for greatly improved efficiency.

August 13, 1964. KPRC-TV begins transmitting from 1,549-foot tower supporting a structure known as "Candelabra," located at Blue Ridge, near DeWalt.

June 3, 1965. The National Aeronautic and Space Administration begins controlling the Gemini series of space flights from the new Manned Spacecraft Center at Clear Lake, and KPRC-TV handles the pool network origination for all networks, as it does for every succeeding Gemini flight through Gemini 12, November 11–15, 1966, and for the Apollo series which follows. Under the pool arrangement, the three domestic networks — NBC, ABC, and CBS — rotate responsibility for the network originations from the Kennedy Space Center at Cape Canaveral, Florida, and the Manned Spacecraft Center at

Clear Lake. All three networks, however, retain KPRC-TV to handle actual originations from Clear Lake.

September 1966. KPRC-TV begins telecasting its local live and film programs, including news film, in color. With network programs already in color, all Channel 2 programs now in color.

October 11, 1968. KPRC-TV originates network pool coverage of *Apollo 7* — the first manned Apollo flight.

December 21, 1968. KPRC-TV originates network pool coverage of *Apollo 8* — the first manned flight to circle the moon.

March 3, 1969. KPRC-TV originates network pool coverage of *Apollo 9* — first rehearsal in space of undocking and docking lunar module with command module.

May 18, 1969. KPRC-TV originates network pool coverage of *Apollo 10* — first rehearsal in lunar orbit of undocking and docking, with lunar module descending to within nine miles of moon's surface.

July 16, 1969. KPRC-TV originates network pool coverage of *Apollo 11* — the first landing by man on the moon.

November 14, 1969. KPRC-TV originates network pool coverage of *Apollo 12* — the second manned exploration of the moon's surface.

April 11, 1970. KPRC-TV originates network pool coverage of *Apollo 13* — a mission aborted because of service module failure. KPRC-TV also provides crew for network pool coverage of "down-range" pickup in the Pacific by the carrier *Iwo Jima.*

September 1970. KPRC-TV participates in first Jerry Lewis Telethon for Muscular Dystrophy. Dick Gottlieb serves as master of ceremonies for this and succeeding telethons in 1971 and 1972; Steve Smith handles 1973 telethon; and Ron Stone becomes "permanent" host in 1974.

January 31, 1971; July 26, 1971; April 16, 1972; December 7, 1972. KPRC-TV originates network pool coverage of flights of *Apollo 14, Apollo 15, Apollo 16,* and *Apollo 17.*

March 1972. KPRC-TV and KPRC move into present quarters at 8181 Southwest Freeway. With three studios, four control rooms, and some 82,000 square feet of space, new plant is considered to be finest local station television facility in world. Cost: approximately $4.5 million.

November 1972. KPRC-TV puts into service its first RCA TCR-100, a semi-automated cartridge playback machine.

October 15, 1975. Channel 2 Television Company purchases WLAC-TV, Nashville, Tennessee. Call letters changed to WTVF (TV).

July 1977. KPRC-TV's weather radar system destroyed by fire. Replaced with new system with 250,000 watts power.

March 1979. At direct request of Bob Hope, KPRC-TV produces first of two telethons for the Hughen School for the Handicapped in Port Arthur. Bob Hope is featured in program produced entirely in our studios.

June 16, 1979. KPRC-TV installs two new Harris BT25L2 transmitters at Blue Ridge plant.

August 14, 1979. KPRC-TV arranges to monitor all National Weather Radars on the Gulf Coast, with locations in Miami, Tampa, Mobile, Slidell (Louisiana), Galveston, and Brownsville. Now possible to monitor any hurricane in the Gulf of Mexico.

November 1979. KPRC-TV builds new mobile unit and equips it with GE cameras.

August 1980. KPRC-TV puts into service five Ampex one-inch color cameras; in August 1981, adds four more for total of nine.

August 7, 1980. KPRC-TV joins other Houston television stations in first of two "Blood Donor" telethons.

October 1, 1981. KPRC-TV begins to receive NBC network service via satellite. Channel 2 had assisted in research leading to NBC's conversion to satellite transmission and received in return as gift "C" band dish antenna used in research.

July 12, 1982. Channel 2 Television Company buys KVOA-TV, Tucson, Arizona.

December 2, 1983. The Houston Post is sold.

December 15, 1983. KPRC-TV and KHTV (Channel 39) begin construction of new 2,049-foot tower. Star Mount top will permit spacing of antennas fifty feet apart.

June 1984. H & C Communications, Inc., is organized and assumes ownership and operation of KPRC-TV and KPRC Radio, WTVF (TV) and KVOA-TV, and completes purchase of WESH-TV, Daytona Beach-Orlando, and KCCI-TV, Des Moines.

December 1, 1984. KPRC-TV puts into service the first satellite news gathering vehicle in Houston, and joins Conus group of stations similarly equipped. Station can now originate and/or receive live satellite transmission from any point in continental United States.

April 20, 1985. KPRC-TV begins transmitting from new 2,049-foot tower.

August 1986. H & C Communications, Inc., completes purchase of KSAT-TV, San Antonio.

Stay tuned.

The original Channel 2 Lynn Coach mobile unit set up at a Houston high school sta-dium for a 1949 football game.

The Lynn Coach mobile unit and original GE camera system on display at the down-town Houston Coliseum.

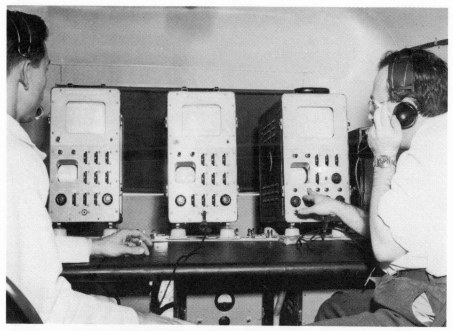

The rudimentary mobile control room set up to handle three cameras from the original Lynn Coach in 1950.

A display of early-model television receivers set up by Channel 2 to help attract audiences.

The equipment display and the crowd that gathered for the big Channel 2 television fair held at the Plantation Club in 1950.

The Plantation Club Television Fair of 1950 served two purposes: to interest people in buying television receivers and to promote the new ownership and call sign of the station, KPRC-TV, Channel 2 in Houston, owned and operated by the Houston Post.

Alfred Daniel, Houston's first radio announcer.

The original Channel 2 quonset hut control room located in the studios at Pin Oak Stables.

Chief engineer Paul Huhndorff, in coat and tie, supervises an early videocast from the old quonset hut at Pin Oak Stables, 1950.

Channel 2's first Houston-Fearless camera dolly at work in the original quonset hut studio at Pin Oak Stables, 1950.

The ladies of "Fashions in Motion" do their final touch-up before going on the air live in the early 1950s.

The new KPRC-TV building complex under construction on Post Oak Road in 1952. Today the entire area of the photograph has been developed as The Galleria and The Lakes on Post Oak. The jog in the two-lane blacktop road at top right is the intersection of today's Post Oak Boulevard and Westheimer.

Another view of the KPRC-TV and Radio complex under construction in 1952. The intersection of Post Oak and Westheimer is at top left.

The "big" studio under construction at the new home of Channel 2 television on Post Oak Road in 1952. This studio, a converted quonset hut, was more than twice the size of Channel 2's first studio.

Equipment from the original Channel 2 studio is unloaded at the new 3014 Post Oak Road location after a midnight move from the original location.

Engineers race against a sunrise deadline to get the just transferred switching equipment reinstalled for the first early-morning telecast from Channel 2's new state-of-the-art facility on Post Oak Road, March 20, 1953.

The view of KPRC-TV and Radio's newly combined facility as seen from Post Oak Road in early 1953.

Part of the crowd of Houstonians that gathered for KPRC-TV's grand open house at the new broadcast studio on Post Oak Road in March 1953.

Thousands of people stood in line for hours to tour the new Channel 2 studios complex in 1953.

General Manager Jack Harris on the left and Governor William P. Hobby, owner of the Houston Post Company, get ready to go live during the telecast of a special program inaugurating the new studio complex in 1953.

Governor William P. Hobby reads greetings from a cue card during a special program inaugurating telecasts from the new Channel 2 studios in early 1953.

Master of ceremonies Dick Gottlieb holds the microphone while Governor William P. Hobby receives best wishes by telephone from the president of NBC-TV.

General manager Jack Harris speaks to the television audience from the new studios of Houston's Channel 2 during special inaugural programming in early 1953.

The "entertainers" on Houston's Channel 2 burst into song from the new studios in early 1953. At the piano is Eddie Aguilar. The singers are, from left, Howard Hartman, Johnny Royal, Janet Smith, Bob Dundas, and Bobby Lahr.

The TuneSchmitts were a staple of early Houston television. Paul Schmitt, band leader, is on the accordion. Dick Shannon is playing the clarinet; behind him to the left is guitar player Felix Stagno; the bass player is Purl Vickers; and singers are Marietta Marich and Bob Russell.

The view south along Post Oak Road toward Channel 2's studios as the station conducted a Lighthouse for the Blind telethon in 1953. The line of cars snakes through the intersection of Post Oak and Westheimer and into the distant KPRC-TV parking lot, where the first "drive in — drop in" contribution barrels were set up.

The head of the line at the June 1953 Lighthouse for the Blind telethon conducted by Channel 2. "Friday Night Wrestling" announcer Paul Boesch is at the car window with a cub scout volunteer.

Master of ceremonies Dick Gottlieb, Houston Lions Club telethon chairman Ray Elliott, and Channel 2's general manager Jack Harris celebrate going "over-the-top" in another early 1950s telethon success.

"Matinee" was telecast from Channel 2 every weekday afternoon during the 1950s. This view is from the seldom-used sponsors' booth above the control room.

The set for Channel 2's evening news was purely functional back in the 1950s.

An early promotional photo for Channel 2's "Friday Night Wrestling." The camera operator hovering over the ring is Gene Lewis. Paul Boesch, announcer and promoter, is holding the microphone inside the ring.

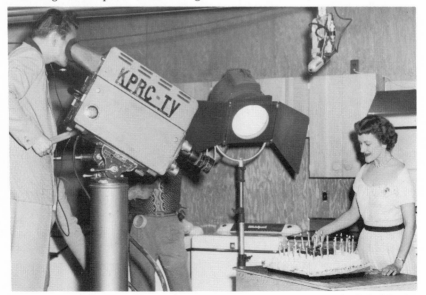

Jane Christopher of the popular "TV Kitchen" celebrates with a studio-baked birthday cake in 1953.

Channel 2 staffers watch the progress of Hurricane Carla on weather radar as it approaches the Texas coast in September 1961.

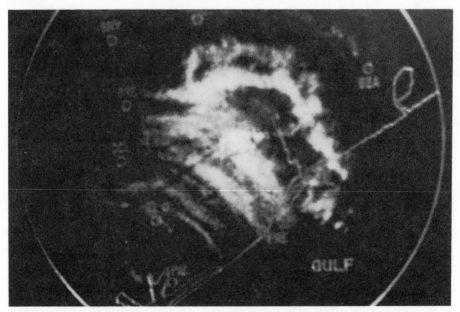

Weather radar view of Hurricane Carla as it hovers over Galveston Island, September 1961.

Still frames from the newsfilm captured by Channel 2 News cameraman Tom Jarriel as Hurricane Carla savaged the beachfront at Galveston, 1961.

The Channel 2 mobile unit put together for the location filming of the documentary program about then Vice-President Lyndon Johnson in 1963.

Lady Bird Johnson and Channel 2 director Bob Marich wait for the cameras to roll during a tour of Vice-President Johnson's LBJ Ranch Home. The tour was conducted by Mrs. Johnson as part of the 1963 documentary on Lyndon Johnson. The assassination of President John F. Kennedy before the show was telecast prevented the airing as edited. However, segments of the program were aired by all three networks and international news organizations in the first days of LBJ's presidential administration.

The Channel 2 remote camera recording Vice-President Johnson's arrival at the LBJ ranch by aircraft — an unscheduled piece of action that almost caused the documentary of Johnson to be cancelled in mid-shoot.

Channel 2's state-of-the-art remote equipment lined up in front of the brand new Astrodome in 1965.

Cameraman John Buffington operates the GE color camera from the Astrodome's fifty-yard line during telecast of an early Houston Oiler football game.

Weatherman John Wissinger and news anchor Ray Miller worked with chalk, chalkboards, and Polaroid snapshots as Houston's Channel 2 began the 1950s.

Jack Valenti, adviser to the Johnson White House, joins Houston Post *columnist Bill Roberts and moderator Ray Miller for a late-night roundtable discussion on the program "The Last Word."*

Ray Miller and Frank Dobbs joined the crew of the SS Manhattan *for the first and only tanker voyage through the Northwest Passage from New York harbor to Prudhoe, Alaska, in the autumn of 1969. Their multiple award-winning documentary film, "Passage to Prudhoe," was exhibited all over the world and even had a special screening in the halls of Congress.*

In 1964 Channel 2 in Houston began telecasting from this 1,549-foot tower at Blue Ridge south of the city.

Channel 2's 1970s model state-of-the-art telecast facility at 8181 Southwest Freeway, designed and constructed to last out the century.

Mrs. Oveta Culp Hobby, Texas Lieutenant Governor Bill Hobby, his wife Diana, and former President Lyndon Johnson take a tour of the new Southwest Freeway studio complex under the guidance of chief engineer Paul Huhndorff.

Gary James and Bill Springer, the two "graybeards" who have been responsible for the pictures and stories on Channel 2's "The Eyes of Texas," one of America's longest-running syndicated television series. James has been producing the show since it went on the air in 1969.

Houston's Channel 2 and Channel 39 have operated from this transmission tower at 2,049 feet above sea level since April 1985.

The Southwest Freeway Radio and Television production headquarters of KPRC-TV and Radio in the mid-1980s after the addition of multiple satellite dish antennas and a helicopter pad.

Voted Houston's most popular anchorman in 1988, Ron Stone reports the story live from distant locations with the help of NEWSSTAR 2, a remote unit able to transmit sound and picture from literally anywhere on earth through satellite relay.

Some of the hundreds of state, national, and international broadcast awards collected by Houston's Channel 2 during forty years of public service telecasting to southeast Texans.

Emcee Ron Stone, former Channel 2 general manager Jack Harris, current vice-president for programming Red Koch, and general manager Tom Reiff smile broadly following word of the grand total for the 1987 Houston effort for the Jerry Lewis Telethon for Neuromuscular Diseases.

The 1988 version of the Channel 2 News set in Studio Three of the KPRC-TV Pro-duction Complex at 8181 Southwest Freeway. As always with Channel 2, the news comes first . . . but in a vastly different way than in those first days forty years ago.

Dan O'Rourke and Ted Shaw

Morning news anchor Dan O'Rourke

Index